# Shaftesbury

# Shaftesbury

*Fighter for the Poor*

Joan Clifford

Marshall Pickering
*An Imprint of HarperCollinsPublishers*

Marshall Pickering is an Imprint of
HarperCollins*Religious*
Part of HarperCollins*Publishers*
77–85 Fulham Palace Road, London W6 8JB

First published in Great Britain
in 1993 by Marshall Pickering

1 3 5 7 9 10 8 6 4 2

Copyright © 1993 Joan Clifford

Joan Clifford asserts the moral right to be
identified as the author of this work

A catalogue record for this book is
available from the British Library

ISBN 0 551 02625 1

Phototypeset by Intype, London
Printed and bound in Great Britain by
HarperCollinsManufacturing Glasgow

CONDITIONS OF SALE

This book is sold subject to the condition that it
shall not, by way of trade or otherwise, be lent, re-sold,
hired out or otherwise circulated without the publisher's
prior consent in any form of binding or cover other
than that in which it is published and without a
similar condition including this condition being
imposed on the subsequent purchaser.

All rights reserved. No part of this publication may be
reproduced, stored in a retrieval system, or transmitted
in any form or by any means, electronic, mechanical,
photocopying, recording or otherwise, without the prior
written permission of the publishers.

For the young people of the Ely Circuit

# ACKNOWLEDGEMENTS

The author wishes to express appreciation for the assistance given by:

Miss Janet Barratt for research; Mr A. D. K. Hawkyard, MA, FRHS, Archivist of Harrow School, and Mr Christopher Mansell, MA.

The following books were particularly helpful:

*Shaftesbury: A Biography of the Seventh Earl*, Georgina Battiscombe, Constable 1974

*Shaftesbury*, G. F. A. Best, Batsford 1964

*The Seventh Earl of Shaftesbury*, Geoffrey B. A. M. Finlayson, Eyre Methuen 1981

*Lord Shaftesbury*, J. L. and Barbara Hammond, Pelican 1939

*The Life and Work of the Seventh Earl of Shaftesbury*, Edwin Hodder, Cassell & Co. 1886 (3 volumes)

*Shaftesbury: The Poor Man's Earl*, John Pollock, Lion 1990

*Victoria R.I.*, Elizabeth Longford, Weidenfeld & Nicolson 1964

*The Great Hunger*, Cecil Woodham Smith, Penguin 1991

# CONTENTS

# PROLOGUE

A boy of about fourteen, a pupil at the famous public school nearby, was walking alone down Harrow Hill in the year 1815.

He was thinking his thoughts, perhaps about his hero Wellington, the famous soldier who had recently defeated the French Emperor Napoleon on the battlefield of Waterloo and had now been created a Duke.

As the boy walked on, he was startled by a disturbance. This was not the sound of carriages rattling by or of street sellers or of people in animated conversation. Round the corner of the street staggered four or five roughly-dressed young men, little older than himself, singing noisily in a drunken manner as they reeled along. They were supporting, or doing their worst to support, a crudely-made wooden coffin. As they lurched under its slight weight, their burden slid to the group with a bump.

The watching schoolboy stood mesmerized by this unexpected and awful sight. He had probably never seen a coffin before, certainly not one travelling along a public street in this way. He knew that when people in his family, usually older members, had died, funerals had been grand, dignified affairs; there had been special black carriages, drawn by black horses with black plumes on their heads, and many relatives going to mourn. These relations would be draped in black clothes and veils and would return afterwards to the house for a quiet family meal. All would be very proper and solemn.

As the men lifted their former comrade they came out with a string of oaths. Showing no respect at all for the deceased friend they were taking to the cemetery, they shuffled on, swaying and cursing as they moved away. Their loud laughter and bawdy songs could be heard growing fainter until they disappeared from sight.

The Harrow schoolboy was horrified. "Can this be permitted simply because the dead man was poor and friendless?" he gasped. He was filled with disgust and pity. Probably it was at this moment, young as he was, that his heart was moved with a feeling for poor people, known generally then as "paupers", for whom poverty meant, among other deprivations, a loss of dignity even at the end of their lives.

Years afterwards he certainly believed that the sight of the pauper funeral had made a striking difference to the future course of his own life.

# 1.

# UNLOVED IN GROSVENOR SQUARE

The boy who witnessed the pauper funeral on Harrow Hill was known as a child as Anthony. He was the eldest son of a noble family, the Ashley Coopers, whose Earldom had been created in 1672. In Anthony's childhood the then Earl was his uncle, his father's elder brother, whose family house or "seat" was at St Giles in Dorsetshire. In years to come, Anthony would come to love this old house. It had once been strongly fortified against enemies and surrounded by a moat. It stood in acres of wooded parkland with fine avenues of trees and had a large lake and a sparkling stream and a shell grotto in the pleasure grounds.

The Ashley Coopers were proud of their ancient lineage and distinguished ancestors. The family bore their own coat of arms and their own motto – "Love, Serve". The name of Ashley Cooper was well known among the English aristocracy, and Anthony's parents were very much part of upper-class society. Yet in spite of all this, the Ashley Cooper children were not happy in the family mansion in London's Grosvenor Square, nor in the country estates of their parents.

The plain truth is that the nine children of Cropley and Anne Ashley Cooper were not really wanted. Their father and mother considered them a nuisance and wearisome responsibility, and easily overlooked them.

These were the days of large families, before family planning was thought about. It was necessary for noble families to have a son and heir, to whom their name and property could be passed. After three girls had arrived, Anthony's birth must have been something of a relief to his father, who needed his heir, but he was not loving to his son. Throughout his life their relationship was never very satisfactory, never very warm, though Anthony longed for a real father's affection.

In those days nearly two hundred years ago, well-to-do families did not see much of their children. By day the children lived in nurseries and schoolrooms with their nurses and governesses or tutors; as the boys grew older they went off to boarding school. As young children they would be carefully dressed in fine clothing, well washed and brushed, and brought

16

down to see their parents in the drawing-room for an hour or so at tea-time, perhaps to be displayed to guests, rather like pets or toys. Then they would be despatched back to the nursery.

So it is clear that Anthony and his sisters, and later the five brothers who came after him, received little loving family life. Not for them the times of rollicking with their parents; very little interest was shown in their activities and hardly any affection displayed. Even in those days when children were expected to be "seen and not heard", the life of the Ashley Cooper children was a tough, harsh regime.

Anthony was born at the beginning of the nine-teenth century, in 1801, when the King was George III. This century was going to be important in Britain. There would be immense changes in manufacturing methods, as a result of many wonderful inventions. Steam-power would bring enormous changes and alter people's lifestyles. Britain would in time grow very prosperous and indeed would rule much of the world and be called "Great". But there would be many problems, and in some of these Anthony would later be much involved.

As a tiny child he naturally did not know any of this. He knew only that, like his brothers

17

and sisters, he was often unhappy, not being able to run in a normal way to his parents. The children were often afraid of their father. He had a job – unpaid, of course, for gentlemen were not supposed to "work" – in the House of Lords, and was considered a capable Chairman of Committees. At home he was something of a bully and spoke brusquely to people, especially his children, who as far as possible kept out of his way. It was not unknown for him to lift his hand to them.

The children's high-born mother, a Duke's daughter, enjoyed a life of party-going and following the social calendar, and had small interest in her children. There was therefore very little of the atmosphere of a true home in the family house and this had an affect on the character and nature of the children. It made Anthony rather shy and lacking in confidence, having only older sisters or small brothers during his childhood.

In later life, he used to say that sometimes the children had even gone hungry, despite the style in which their parents lived, for the servants were careless about meal times. Sometimes the children were cold, if the coal scuttles had not been refilled. Nobody seems to have made sure the servants were reliable. It was a miserable life for the children.

Fortunately for Anthony, there was a gleam of light in his life. This shone from a lady called Maria Milles. She had first worked as lady's maid to the children's mother, but on retirement from this position she stayed on in the household. She had been with the family for a long time and seems to have had some authority, perhaps as housekeeper. She was entrusted with the care of little Anthony and as a small child he found in her the love and tenderness denied him from his mother.

Probably Maria encouraged the little boy in his reading. She also helped him in a more important way that made all the difference to his life. Apart from the fact that Anthony found in her someone who actually cared about him, Maria was a Christian and passed on to the little boy her Christian faith. Hers was not a sophisticated theology. She was a simple believer in a clear, straightforward Christian message – the love of God for each individual, the saving grace of Jesus, the power of the Scriptures and of personal prayer. So she taught young Anthony the Bible stories and he came easily to grasp that Maria exemplified in her life the virtues and graces that he saw in the life of Jesus. Anthony was devoted to her and in their happy relationship his life and personality blossomed.

During the times he spent with Maria he was a happy little boy, basking in her affection. And in his young heart, he accepted the Christian Gospel that she had offered him, and this stood him in good stead all through his life. His own religious beliefs would always be like hers – simple, direct, straightforward and very personal – known as "evangelical". He would never be much interested in the rituals of the church, in elaborate church practices or the robing of priests. Indeed in adult life he was often rather critical of the clergy and bishops, though he was always looking for greater numbers of parish clergy to spread the faith.

Anthony was very young when he received these Christian truths from Maria and no one knows whether in his teenage years he underwent any dramatic religious conversion. It seems as though the teaching and example of Maria directly touched his heart and soul and were sufficient to convince him that this was the right way to live. He went on from there.

When Anthony was seven he was sent away to school. This proved to be as miserable an existence as staying at home. The school was a large and well known one, called Manor House, at Chiswick, not a great way from the family's country home at Richmond on the River Thames. At one time the school had been well run and satisfactory. Now, however, the headmaster, Dr Horne, was getting old. He relied a good deal for discipline on beating. Years afterwards, when Anthony was grown up, he remembered all this very clearly. He remembered the neglect of both the buildings and the boys, for the living quarters were dirty and unkempt and the food poor. There was also that horror of most children, especially the young and sensitive, bullying. ''There was hard treatment of every sort'', he would recall.

There was little to commend the Chiswick school, except perhaps that it opened Anthony's eyes to misery to such an extent that he could later easily understand other people's worries and sorrows in a remarkable way. Fortunately, when he now needed support, the encouraging words and prayers of Maria Milles upheld him. Her Christian message and the belief she had given him that God did love him came to his rescue, and helped the little boy to endure the unpleasant years spent at his first school. He said his prayers daily as he had been taught.

At least during the school holidays he could see Maria, running to tell her his thoughts and troubles and throwing his arms round her and receiving the same unaltering affection that made him happy. He also enjoyed holiday games with his brothers and sisters – well out of the way of their parents, who were liable to find fault and growl at them whenever they were sighted.

Sadly, when Anthony was only ten, Maria fell ill and died. This was a great blow to him and he was never even told where she had been buried. She had been like a true mother to him and he felt wretched and very lonely. To his delight she had remembered him in her simple Will and had left him a gold watch. Anthony cherished this and wore it all through his life, saying he liked it better than any other. It must have been of a good size and had perhaps belonged to Maria's father, a worker on the great estate at Blenheim Palace. The boy thought the world of the gold watch, and in years to come would often show it proudly to people, saying, "This belonged to the best friend I ever had."

When he was eleven years old, important changes occurred in the Ashley Cooper family. His uncle, the Fifth Earl, died and Anthony's father succeeded to the title and became known as the Sixth Earl of Shaftesbury.

From that time onward, Anthony, as the

eldest son of the family, was always known as Ashley, part of the continuing family name. His baby days were over.

## 2.

# HAPPIER DAYS AND IDLE HOURS

Things took a happier turn for Ashley when, at thirteen, he was sent to Harrow school. Here as a boarder, away from the miseries of Manor House and the bleakness of home, he felt more cheerful. He was still a comparatively quiet boy and, apart from a reasonable scholastic record, little was remarked about him during his years at the school. His time there, though, was something he would remember as important, both for friendships made and new opportunities, and also for the charismatic effect of his stumbling across the pauper funeral.

Harrow was not the school his father had attended but was already very famous. The original school building had been completed in 1615 and when Ashley enrolled there were over two hundred pupils. The boys did not wear a uniform and had not then adopted the straw "boater" which later identified them. The Founder of the school was John Lyon and the school arms showed a lion rampant with crossed arrows. The school motto was *Donorum dei dispensatio fidelis*, translated from the Latin as "The faithful stewardship of the gifts of God". The phrase was to become very appropriate to Ashley himself in the future.

The Head of the school was Dr Butler, a fine man, accomplished and civilized. Some ex-pupils whom Ashley would know or recognize in later life included the poet Lord Byron and statesmen Sir Robert Peel and Lord Palmerston. When Ashley was handed over to the care of the school, his father remarked gruffly that he had knocked the boy down and recommended the tutors to do the same! This may have been an example of heavy humour on the part of Ashley's father but it was hardly a good start. On the whole, Ashley had more to stand up to from the boys than from the tutors.

Ashley began to enjoy his new life and to develop well. He grew tall and strong and took his part in various athletic pursuits. Cricket was played and boxing encouraged – of the bare-fist form in those days. Ashley could put up a good show and became quite a formidable opponent.

The school had a strong classical tradition

and the boys spent long hours poring over their Latin primers in the panelled schoolroom. In the winter "lock-up" was at 6pm and the boys were then bursting with suppressed energy and ready for any prank. Some relished the diversion of secretly stealing out of school in the evening. They would climb down a rope from the upper windows of their boarding house and help each other to scale an awkward twelve-foot wall. Then – freedom! They would rush across the fields for a game of Jack O'Lantern – a sort of teenage hide and seek in which they would scramble across the dark muddy fields by the flashing light of the distant lantern. Later there was the excitement of feeling their way back into school without being seen.

There was not much supervision of activities outside of school hours and since this was a rough age, the boys – in spite of the aristocratic background of most of them – could be tough characters. In winter sessions of hard snowballing, the snowball might well contain a stone! Life at Harrow could be a toughening process but it did not affect Ashley adversely. He learned to stand up for himself.

He also had good companions, his chief friend being Harry Verney of Claydon who would in time marry the sister of the famous Florence Nightingale. Ashley won some prizes

– his good brain was beginning to work well. He got into the Under VI form before he was fifteen. And he was discovered to have a sense of humour.

Yet, young as he was, moments of depression engulfed him, as they were to do all his life, when he felt low in spirit and nothing could cheer him.

The aristocratic pupils among whom he moved did not find much time to think about the poor, who in the future would so much concern Ashley. The poor were regarded as social inferiors and little bothered about. After all, the boys seldom came into contact with them. This was largely true of Ashley also. But he no doubt continued to say his prayers and to attend school chapel. God was working in his heart to produce the young man who later would think very much about the underprivileged of the nation and would take their problems on himself.

Ashley's happy days at Harrow were rather brief. After three years he was told that he had to leave. It was probably a matter of expense. Although his father had inherited the Shaftesbury Earldom, he had not been left huge wealth as the bulk of the family fortune had been left to the former Earl's daughter. Thus, although Cropley Ashley Cooper had inherited the great family properties, the finances to maintain them were not overlarge. And now he had these big estates to look after. Probably the fees of Harrow school for his son were not a priority. At any rate, he told Ashley that he must leave and that was that. Ashley probably shrugged his shoulders – he was accustomed by now to his father's unpredictable behaviour.

It was now decided, the boy learned, that he was to spend a year or two living with a relative before his adult life unfolded. He was sent to live for two years with his cousin and her clergyman husband. This was the establishment of the Reverend Frederick Ricketts, Rector of Eckington near Chesterfield, and of his wife. Ashley fully realized that his father did not want to have any real relationship with him and that he was being sent to Derbyshire largely to be "got out of the way". It was not encouraging.

The Derbyshire rectory was no doubt stylish and comfortable. Since the young cleric confessed frankly that he was not able to teach Ashley anything, it does not seem that he was any kind of scholar. It is likely that, as was often the way in those days, he was the younger son of gentry, sent into the church as a profession. These gentlemen were often under the patronage of nobility, and had not always entered the priesthood because of a burning sense of vocation. They would perform their church duties and live comfortably, often in the country, riding to hounds, shooting, and visiting the local gentry. It was an agreeable if undramatic life.

Thus Ashley would not find his new home unpleasant but could not expect much to come out of it. Nor did it. He freely admitted, later in life, that it was a pleasant interlude, for his father expected nothing from his hosts in Derbyshire but that they would "keep an eye" on Ashley for the next two years. So for the time being the teenage boy enjoyed the life of a young country gentleman, doing very little studying. As he later said, "I hardly ever opened a book." It did not seem to occur to him that after some scholastic successes at Harrow this was disappointing. He was given a horse and enjoyed a day's hard riding. He went for long walks with the family dogs – he was always fond of dogs.

There was constant visiting between the local families, and neighbours were kind and welcoming to the young Ashley, inviting him to their drawing-rooms, to their receptions and balls. He was now sixteen and had grown into a good-looking youth. He was tall, indeed still growing, well-built yet graceful, with a good upright carriage. He had thick black curly hair, strong features and deep-set blue eyes. He had pleasing manners and was beginning to develop social graces. People liked to have him around and found him a pleasant companion. Ladies thought him charming. Ashley found it delightful to be welcomed in this way – indeed to have any attention paid to him at all. The ambitious thoughts that had sometimes flitted into his mind at Harrow disappeared. He agreed in later life that he had been, at this time, ''bone idle''.

Yet sometimes, in the odd moment, what he later called "all sorts of aspirations" floated into his mind. It could have been that these were the ambitions of most young men, then and now, to become famous and important and perhaps wealthy. Or it could have been that he recalled the day of the pauper funeral and the concern for poor people that it aroused. Whatever these aspirations were, they did not bear fruit for many years to come.

To Ashley's delight, his father had opened up the great family mansion in Dorset. In breaks from his life in Derbyshire, Ashley was able to roam the house and grounds, still avoiding his parents. He grew to love the house, St Giles, which he called "the dear old Saint". He always held the deepest of feelings for this old house and it was to be to him both a splendid joy and a fearful responsibility. But now he would ramble in the parklands and explore long corridors and rooms he had never seen before. He knew that one day this old mansion would be his and his family's and the thought thrilled him.

Although Ashley would in future do so much to help poor people and fight for a better life for them, he was convinced of the rightness of the social order of his time: God had placed some people in aristocratic families and some in lowly ones and it was nobody's right to question this. He believed that the nobility possessed prosperity and power to exercise well and in a kindly manner, and that the working poor should be properly respectful to their "betters" – but be helped by them to live decent lives. The idea of democracy and of ordinary people getting a vote and influencing the government of the country would have seemed quite extraordinary to him and he could never approve of this. He had intense pride in his aristocratic background and ancient lineage. He was simply in these respects a child of his time.

In years to come, Ashley would live through

times of tension, even near-revolution that would lap the shores of Britain as it had overflowed in France and threatened other countries. There were already in England rumblings of discontent among poor people who were caught up in the immense industrial changes in the land. Before Ashley had even gone to Harrow, Luddite Riots had taken place, when manual workers afraid for their jobs had stolen up on the factories at night and smashed the new machinery in the workshops.

In 1816 such discontent showed a menacing aspect. At first in East Anglia, groups of workers crept together at night to plan disturbances; they sent threatening letters and set houses, barns and rick-yards on fire. There was a poor harvest and unemployment was widespread. Small but influential bands of agitators were stirring things up among the working people and talking openly of revolution. A mob stormed a gunsmith's shop in London but ran off when troops were sighted.

The plain truth was that the old-accustomed social order, where those at the top, mostly aristocrats, gave the orders and the people below unquestioningly obeyed these orders, was over. Society was stirring in a determined way and things would never be the same again. There would be many struggles, both inside

Parliament and out among the people, and into this struggle Ashley would be plunged.

But at this moment, as a sixteen-year-old youth, he had no notion of this. He thought only that, after years of comparative misery, life was at the moment rather pleasant.

## 3.

# A YOUNG MAN OF PRIVILEGE

Arguments raged in the family mansion. How should Ashley begin his adult life? What was to be the next step after leaving his cousin's rectory? His father decreed that Ashley should go into the army, into a good regiment.

Ashley was not at all keen on this, despite his admiration for the Duke of Wellington and the fact that he himself, on his mother's side, was descended from the famous soldier Marlborough. He did not wish to become a soldier, he had always hated war.

Fortunately, even his father could sometimes be persuaded against his own wishes. A family friend, sensing Ashley's unhappiness, talked seriously to the Earl and finally it was agreed that Ashley should not be forced to adopt a military career. What then? It was agreed that he should go to university, to the old college of his father and grandfather – Christ Church, Oxford. So in 1819 he went up.

When his father inherited the family Earldom, Ashley, then aged eleven, received the title of "Lord". But his friends at Harrow had not bothered much with this, it being not unusual there. Now he was entering the adult world and he became known as "Lord Ashley". As a titled undergraduate at Oxford he was expected to wear a "tuft", a gold-tasselled cap, as a sign of social superiority. He saw nothing wrong in this.

Christ Church, founded by King Henry VIII on a scheme of Cardinal Wolsey, was always known as "the House". It had an aristocratic and political reputation and was one of the largest and wealthiest colleges in Oxford. It was a delightful place in which to be an undergraduate, truly a place of privilege.

The buildings were splendid. Tom Gate housed the bell called Great Tom. One side of the college bordered on the meadow leading down to the River Cherwell. It was a pleasant walk down to the banks. Between there and Tom Quad were the cathedral cloisters from which you entered the Cathedral. The thirteenth-century spire was the first to be built in England. The Cathedral itself was famous for its vaulted roof and fine windows.

Christ Church had many famous "sons" and Ashley would be followed there by William

Gladstone, who graduated in 1831 and later became Prime Minister.

Christ Church was proud of its church traditions and most of the teaching staff were unmarried clergymen. There were, of course, no women students so women were rarely seen within the College.

Ashley discovered that his cousin, Edward Pusey, had come up to the House at the same time. They were never very close, largely because of differing religious views, which mattered a lot to both of them. Pusey was to devote his life to the restoration of Catholic worship in the Church of England. He would in later life become a Canon of the Cathedral where he had worshipped as an undergraduate. Since Ashley was slowly forming his own very personal religious views, which were known as "evangelical", and disliked the rituals so important to Pusey, their relationship was awkward.

Ashley was glad to make a lasting friendship with George Howard, who afterwards became the Earl of Carlisle. Like Ashley, George was rather a quiet young man, not at all flamboyant. He was very shy and sometimes got left behind in the social activities to which Ashley grew more attracted. Ashley was determined to "bring out" George socially. He took him to

visit friends, and George was overcome with
shyness outside the door, hesitating to go into
the drawing-room. Shyness gave way to laughter when Ashley dramatically flung open the
big double doors and called out very loudly, in
the manner of a liveried servant – "The
Honourable George Howard."

"Tufts", as the young aristocrats were
known, led active social lives and paid little
attention to their studies as a rule. But both
George and Ashley had made up their minds
to concentrate on their work and to achieve
good honours degrees, which needed much
burning of the midnight oil and real discipline.
This did not prevent Ashley from having a
good time. The young men, with their friends,
took holidays together in the long vacations,
particularly liking to go to Scotland. Even
more, Ashley enjoyed visiting George's family
at their home, Castle Howard, near York. He
was much attracted by George's mother, Lady
Morpeth, a kind, gentle woman who became a
delightful mature friend. She welcomed her
son's friend. He was not at all tongue-tied with
her but found he could talk easily and that
she listened sympathetically. This was such
a contrast with his relationship with his own
mother. He was able to write to Lady Morpeth,
telling her about college life and his views and

opinions, always plentiful in a young man. She, in her turn, tried gently to confront him with his tendency to pass quick, violent judgements on people, not always wisely.

Ashley also found pleasure in the company of George's four pretty sisters, teasing the smallest one and playing various games with her. After all, he had four sisters of his own. From time to time he would fancy himself a little in love with each of the three older girls, but these were innocent happy passing relationships which all recognized. Ashley was always pleased to be at Castle Howard, and the family on their side thought him a delightful companion. Ashley confided in Lady Morpeth that the friendship he and George had begun at Oxford would, he hoped, continue throughout their lives.

Ashley and George did work hard at their studies and took their examinations. Before the oral Ashley was nervous but when called he did well. Both young men achieved the first class honours they had desired.

Some people's lives are clearly marked by their time spent at university; this was not so with Ashley. He had completed his degree course, his brain had awakened and he had achieved his goal. But the atmosphere of the famous old place seems to have had little affect upon his future, though he must have made friends there who would prove influential in his later career. His religious life had not been remarkably vigorous, though he had continued to say his prayers and attend church services and to adhere to the strict standards of living of which he felt Maria Milles would have approved. Her influence never left him.

The relationship between Ashley and his father had not improved. The Earl did not seem to want Ashley's company at all and made it grumpily clear that the young man must find living accommodation of his own. This strange state of affairs was accepted by Ashley who now spent some time visiting friends and generally once again keeping out of his parents' way.

It was decided that he should travel abroad, making the "Grand Tour" as was the custom with young men of good family. With a friend or two, they would catch the packet-boat across the Channel, hire a carriage and pursue a leisurely journey across Europe, staying at various centres of culture such as Paris, Rome, Florence, Athens. Here they went to art galleries and looked at ancient architecture, took long walks and climbs and admired the scenery. They were meant to store their minds with

European culture, essential for their lives as gentlemen and for the conversations they would have with the fair sex. They called on relatives resident abroad and were given useful introductions to notable families, embassies and consulates, and generally made much of. And if they met pretty young women of good family through these introductions, so much the happier. These Grand Tours were a delightful passage between boyhood and man's estate.

On such a tour Ashley now set out, though with a comparatively small allowance rather grudgingly handed out by his father. He was not going to impress anyone by splashing money around.

Ashley was now twenty-two, a good-looking, upright young man with considerable charm and confidence, though sometimes restrained by shyness. He knew that he was subject to unpredictable moods – one day being happy as a lark and the next depressed and morose. This temperamental trait would increasingly be a burden to him. He was also, as Lady Morpeth had pointed out to him, still subject to violent prejudices. But basically he had an attractive personality and he now set out to enjoy himself.

As he travelled in carefree-style across the

Channel, he seems hardly to have realized the simmering nature of the political and social scene at home. Workers were still agitating against their masters, and while Ashley was still at college a terrible event had taken place. Thousands of demonstrators in the northern city of Manchester were being stirred up by a Wiltshire farmer who had upset the police. There was an attempt to arrest him and a riot broke out. Soldiers hastened in and the terrified mob scattered in all directions. There was total panic and violence ensued. One man was killed and about forty hurt. This event became known as the Battle of Peterloo. It boded ill for the peace of the land. The following year a plot was hatched, which failed, to kidnap some cabinet ministers. Politicians became worried that they would lose control of the people and that some kind of bloody revolution would break out.

However, Ashley travelled placidly on with his Oxford friend, anticipating pleasure and excitement.

The excitement occurred when he reached Vienna, a beautiful city then in its imperial heyday, where he fell wildly in love. He found young women attractive and since he was handsome, well connected, courteous and affable, several had mistaken his attentiveness for something deeper. The mothers of these girls in whom he had not really been deeply interested were therefore quite relieved when Ashley left England for a while.

He was now absolutely bowled over. The girl in question was a delightful blonde, Antoinette von Leykam. Unfortunately for Ashley, her family circumstances were thought less than satisfactory. She was the daughter of an Austrian baron, a diplomat, and she was an opera singer – in those days not considered a respectable career for a lady. Because of this the von Leykams were "not received" in snobbish Viennese society. Any official alliance between Ashley and the young Antoinette would have been frowned upon, not only in Vienna but definitely in London by Ashley's parents.

The young lady was also a Roman Catholic; this too would have proved an insurmountable block to marriage with such a dedicated evangelical Church of England Christian as Ashley.

But he was deeply affected by this lovely girl whom he called in his affectionate German, "Liebe, dear Liebe".

Unrewarded love is always painful and Ashley never altogether recovered from his parting with Antoinette. But he accepted that she was not for him. Nobody knows quite how the relationship ended but end it did. The two young people managed to remain friends and later Antoinette married the powerful Austrian statesman Prince Metternich. He was an important enough national figure to marry anyone he pleased and his wife took her place in Vienna's glittering society. Sadly she died young in giving birth to a son.

This interlude grieved Ashley for a long time, but he considered it did help him understand himself better. He faced the fact that he possessed strong sexual feelings and looked forward eagerly to marriage with the right mate. He was always a man of intense emotions and this both gave him much joy and also caused him much suffering.

When Ashley arrived back in England he was more mature. He had been given time for thinking and his Christian faith was becoming more defined. Having yet no settled occupation for his life, he took to studying Christian matters, reading the Bible carefully and thinking about the responsibilities of his future. He also enjoyed his hobbies, particularly astronomy. When star-gazing at the heavens he was conscious of the greatness of God and the smallness of man.

He was not totally serious. When in the mood, he had a good sense of humour and could make others laugh, even the poor old king whom he visited at Windsor. Ashley admitted to liking the social round – the parties and outings and balls arranged in high society. He did not yet anticipate the heavy responsibilities that would come to him.

He commenced a habit that he would keep up all his life, that of writing a diary. Every day he recorded his private thoughts. After his death the diaries became available, to the interest of generations of readers. He sought always to be in control of himself, his temper and his behaviour, but in his diary he "let himself go" and scribbled passionately what he really thought about people and events, sometimes in quite wild words. The diary was a safety valve for an emotional person under strict daily control.

# 4.

# AT WESTMINSTER

Member of Parliament for Woodstock! As the
eldest son of a great family, Ashley now
entered the House of Commons at Westminster – the beginning of a life of public service
there and the beginning of his battles on behalf
of poor people.

Ashley did not have to fight a campaign to
get into the House as men and women later
did, and indeed as he himself was to do later,
going out "on the hustings" and convincing
people that he would be a good candidate. No,
in fact he would have been very surprised not
to have had a seat offered to him. In the early
days of his political career there were many
abuses in the parliamentary system. Many con-
stituencies were at the disposal of rich patrons,
often the Crown, while bribery and corruption
flourished. The mass of the British people had
no vote. Aristocratic families believed they had
a divine right to govern the country and Ashley
was no exception. Coming from a long line of

the ruling classes he accepted it as a heaven-sent right that he should be among them. His own parliamentary seat for Woodstock was the gift of his uncle, the Duke of Marlborough.

So as he entered the House of Commons for the first time in 1826, he would not have had such thoughts as "I am lucky to be here!" – or "I have done well to get this seat!" He would enter with the calm assurance that it was almost pre-ordained. As he looked round the Chamber in which the Members met – at that time St Stephen's Chapel, Westminster – he would see many men he recognized, some relatives, some acquaintances of his parents, most of them solid members of the aristocracy.

He must surely have sometimes looked about him and thought of the dramatic history of Parliament and of the famous and notorious men who had played their part in it.

When he entered Parliament the parties were the Tories (Conservatives) and the Whigs. The Tories sympathized with the rule of privilege and wished to maintain the long established institutions of the country. The Whigs were more radical and sought greater democracy and a widening of the franchise to enable more people to vote.

From his father and friends Ashley had some knowledge of the procedures of the House and knew roughly what to do. But like most young men he was somewhat naïve at first, and got a bit alarmed at the cut and thrust of the debates and the rudeness which was so much against his own nature. At this time he had not really thought through his own political party allegiance in any deep way and just took it for granted that he would naturally agree in all detail with the general principles of the Tory party for which he stood. He later found that this was not so and gradually he became less of a "party man" and more of a straightforward humanitarian. However, during his first days in the House he naturally wished to conform and tried to do so. He was upset by the shouting and the verbal attacks upon his Tory friends and felt enraged – he would rush home and hastily write out all his anger and distress in his private diary.

"What I suffer!" he scribbled, "from the brazen-faced and low insults of the Radical party!" He began to wonder if he had the stamina to stand up to the goings-on in the House, the rough and tumble. Yet he knew that he must.

Was he ambitious? Inwardly he did often feel that he was destined for great things. He believed he had the capacity and he knew that he had some powerful friends, like the Duke of Wellington, who would encourage him. At times – though he would not speak of this to anyone – he even saw himself as a future Prime Minister.

During his early days, other people thought so too. He had so much going for him: brains, good connections, a good presence, influence, charm and a love of his country.

He was also quickly known publicly as a practising Christian. People nodded and held this to be good, though later some Members of the House found his uncompromising attitudes and strict standards rather tiresome. However, at the moment he was a "coming young man". Up to now he had shown no particular concern for the worries of the poor, and in his private life he spent a good deal of time on his hobbies.

Rather to his surprise he was soon given office as a Junior Minister when Wellington became Prime Minister. Ashley was invited to become a Commissioner of the India Board of Control. This was a salaried government job which helped his always precarious finances. He took the job seriously, studied his papers carefully and became deeply interested in the Indian sub-continent and concerned for all that went on there. As a Christian he also longed for India to leave behind its gods Shiva and

Vishnu and turn to the Christian faith. This rather simplistic view did not take into account India's long history and complex issues.

Soon came the first exposure of Ashley's public personality. A new Member of Parliament usually makes a "maiden speech" – meaning his first – and the other Members of the House always pay special attention to this, to find out what kind of orator and presenter this new Member is. It fell to Ashley to make his speech in 1828. He had been asked to be a member of a parliamentary select committee. These were groups of men who spent time away from the debating chamber looking into special topics and deciding whether these topics needed to be made the subject of parliamentary bills.

The committee on which Ashley now sat was somewhat disturbing for a young man, but he grasped the opportunity with both hands and never throughout his long life turned his back on the subject. The cause which was central was that of the "Pauper Lunatics" – in other words, the very poor who were mentally ill.

These were days long before there was much knowledge of the workings of the mind, and even mildly eccentric people could be dubbed "mad". The prospects for mentally-disturbed people if they were rich were not very satisfactory; for the mentally sick poor, conditions were abysmal. There were still those who thought people were "lunatics" because they or their parents had done something bad. Others still believed the mentally ill to be possessed by evil spirits. The main attitude to them was of restraint in case they were a menace to others rather than of understanding their condition and trying to help them. The poor creatures in the mental asylum at Bedlam had a lamentable existence, often tied up in squalid living conditions. At long last the public was being gradually awakened to their distress and made to feel uncomfortable about them. So the select committee met and reported and now the matter had to be brought before the House of Commons to try to enforce better laws.

It was Ashley's difficult task to speak on this subject but he was resolute. He was full of pity for the pauper lunatics. He forced himself to visit several "madhouses", as they were known, and was devastated by the spirit of hopelessness evident and the misery of the demented inmates.

So as he later reported in his diary, he got up in the House for his "first effort for the advance of human happiness". He felt nervous and inexperienced in front of the large audience with every eye turned on him. At first he spoke in a rather low voice, difficult to make out for those at the back. But as he went on he became more confident. He gave a very clear report. He was seconding a Member, asking Parliament to bring in a bill that would appoint Lunacy Commissioners, people who would on behalf of the government make critical inspections of the asylums.

His speech must have been very appealing and touched hearts because the Bill, which had been thrown out once, was now accepted and soon became law.

Ashley had realized by now that people were not always polite at the reading of Bills. Sometimes a motion was carried that a Bill be "rejected and torn", which meant the paper on which the Bill was written was actually torn up. It was even said that a Bill treated like this had been kicked by Members as they left the Commons, so unpopular had it been!

Ashley did not think he had done remarkably well in his first speech but as people crowded round to congratulate him he knew this was not true. He would quickly learn to manage his voice well and mastered some tricks of oratory. He would always be careful in his preparation, not being at his best with *extempore* speaking. Above all, he was at his most powerful when his heart was in his speech, when he cared with passion for his subject.

He now felt very glad that he had been able to do something towards the improvement of life for a miserable group of people, the mentally sick. It was the first step. He was often to find in later years that affairs that began as duties usually led on to be of absorbing interest and total involvement.

So his political life was now under way. He was also now sought after as one of London's eligible bachelors, though one or two people thought him a little eccentric. Society mothers knew that he was not very wealthy. Nor was his plain-spoken Christian witness always appreciated. The court under the reign of "Prinny", now King George IV, was not much bothered with moral issues and the king himself, now in his last days, had never been a setter of standards in society, though he was a patron of the arts. The days of the Regency, soon to pass away, were days of idle living and small concern with religion. Ashley did not feel particularly at home in such surroundings, though he was continually having to learn to accept with some degree of tolerance people of whose lifestyle he did not approve.

Whilst he was anxious not to get romantically entangled, he was very conscious of his need to find a suitable wife and brought this matter into his prayers constantly. He was now nearly thirty years old and wanted to settle down. "Where is the woman?" he asked himself. He was always dreaming of his ideal girl and found it very hard to forget Antoinette, his Viennese love.

# 5.

# A TRUE ROMANTIC

Ashley was determined now to get married.
He recognized his own passionate nature and
had no wish to enter into affairs. He had an
intensely romantic disposition and looked for
all the virtues, plus exquisite beauty and style,
in a future wife. In years to come his wife
would be mistress of Dorset St Giles and would
need to support him in his political life – he
still thought this might include high office –
and would need to be an elegant hostess, tact-
ful in dealing with important people, and a
capable ruler of her household. All this in
addition, inevitably, to motherhood of a large
family.

Most of all, Ashley yearned for a true partner
who would give him the love and affection for
which he so longed, for so long denied to him
in his relations with his parents. Rather prig-
gishly he confided to his diary that he "dreaded
the chance of a Jezebel or a Cleopatra . . ."
Where was the paragon he sought?

He was popular with mothers and daughters who saw him as eligible, being tall and handsome and of good family. At balls and parties and visiting private houses he met numerous pretty girls – well brought up with refined tastes, intended for the life of good society. He was frequently attracted to one or other of them but none seemed quite to fit the bill. He was drawn to the Lady Selina Jenkinson, daughter of Lord Liverpool, but her father discouraged the match. Ashley's rather strait-laced character and poor financial situation were not lost upon fathers.

"Oh my prayer, my prayer, how I repeat it! A wife! A wife!" murmured Ashley dramatically.

Then, during the social round, he set eyes upon the Lady Emily Cowper and found that he very much admired her. She was seventeen when he first met her in 1828, a pretty, vivacious girl with a sunny nature, full of the joys of life. She had indeed been brought up to regard life as a pleasant garden and not to bother much about the serious issues of the day.

Yet, gazing upon her and knowing something of her family background, Ashley would sigh. If Antoinette had been socially unacceptable, other problems would beset him as a possible suitor for the lovely Emily. She was the daughter of Lady Cowper, who was of the Lamb family, somewhat notorious for their free lifestyle. Her father, supposedly Lord Cowper, was thought really to be Lord Palmerston, known to be Lady Cowper's longtime lover. For Ashley, a staunch believer in Christian family virtues, all this was awkward.

Anyway, it was by no means certain that Lady Emily, known to her family and friends as "Minny", would immediately fall into his arms. She was much sought after and it was said she had already refused marriage with four suitors, including Lord John Russell who would one day be Prime Minister. She was enjoying life and had no immediate wish to be tied down. Perhaps she also enjoyed the power she knew she exercised upon impressionable young men.

Ashley's feelings, always easily roused, were in a whirl. He found himself constantly thinking about Minny. "She is lovely, accomplished, clever," he wrote. Within a few months he knew that he was deeply in love. But he also sought to find in his mate one who would share his Christian beliefs and commitments. He yearned to share with this lovely girl "all the sublimities of religion".

It seems unlikely that Minny had been thinking so deeply. Ashley's intensity frightened her a little. Meeting in Tunbridge Wells, they walked out sedately to call upon Princess Lieven. Suddenly, without any warning, Ashley blurted out a proposal of marriage to Minny as they strolled along. Minny was not prepared for this and was confused and would not give a definite answer. At this Ashley became angry and would have stomped off. But Minny, now composed, gently persuaded him to continue their journey and Ashley's anger died away.

All onlookers had by now grasped the fact that Ashley was desperately in love and that some decision had to be reached. It was Lady Cowper's opinion that Minny did not care strongly enough for the young man. Minny's family were of differing opinions concerning the suitor. Her brother William, an Eton schoolboy, told a schoolfriend that Ashley was a man of "energy, earnestness and tenderness". Minny's uncle, however, Sir Patrick Lamb, a man of the world, was in no doubt that anything to do with the Shaftesbury family would be a misfortune for Minny. He wrote to his sister urging her to discourage the match, pointing out Ashley's poor financial prospects, certainly while his father was alive, and stating that Ashley was "odd". Without beating about the bush he exploded that "poor Min" could not expect much from association with a family of "an odious father and four beggarly brothers". He considered the marriage would forge an "undesirable connection".

Poor Ashley! For him the course of true love was not running smoothly. Lady Cowper, not a very decisive woman, could not make up her mind whether to encourage Ashley and Minny or not. Then Minny herself took the upper hand. It seems she decided that she did love Ashley enough to give him her hand and heart and she agreed to marry him. Perhaps the opposition spurred her on. Her family was not overjoyed, nor was Ashley's. His father refused to attend the wedding and was his usual awkward self.

However, Ashley and Minny pressed on with their plans and the wedding was arranged for June 1830 at St George's, Hanover Square, a fashionable London church. Ashley was thrilled at the sight of his lovely young bride and Minny saw her new husband as tall, commanding and handsome. There was a smart reception at Lord Hertford's. Ashley's father, with a quick change of heart, suddenly appeared and circulated with some grace among the guests, for once being amiable to his son.

At the time of her marriage, Minny was young and perhaps not of such a passionate nature as her husband. However, she was soon deeply devoted to him and there began a marriage of true hearts and minds that was to continue for over forty years.

Ashley, for his part, was ecstatic. "O Great God, what a treasure to possess such a darling," he wrote in his diary. In her he found all the love and tenderness he desired. Minny's life as Ashley's wife was not all honey. She was, in the manner of those days, to have a large family of ten children. And although her grand houses would be well-staffed with servants, she and Ashley had no intention of leaving the family to their care. It was particularly important to Ashley that his children, when they came, would have a happier life than he and his siblings had known. This came not from a sense of duty alone, for he truly loved children and was never happier than when they were about him.

Minny also had to come to terms with Ashley's religious views. She had not been brought up to pay much attention to personal religion. But her relatives were people of good manners and sensitive feelings for others and Ashley believed that he could lead Minny into sharing his own Christian beliefs. After all, he reflected, his own sisters had grown up good Christian women and had not been influenced by their selfish mother. He found there were no problems with Minny, who responded wonderfully.

Minny herself was probably not a deep thinker. But she possessed many fine qualities and the vital elements of a sunny nature, not easily pessimistic and not one to throw tantrums or let problems overwhelm her. This was a quality foreign to Ashley and one he could not really cultivate. He was the eternal worrier and always liable to go into gloomy moods. He was to be for ever grateful for Minny's cheerful and lively personality, as well as admiring her beauty and charm.

He could not mould his in-laws into his pattern of views and for their lifetimes he was enmeshed in a rather awkward relationship with them. In time Lady Cowper's husband died and she then married Lord Palmerston. Ashley could not approve of their lifestyle – easy-going and frivolous as he saw it – but he was forced to admit that no two people could have been kinder or more generous to him than these two.

When he was in financial difficulty – an ongoing situation – or needed political support, his mother-in-law and her husband never failed. They were both worldly people, without acknowledged religious beliefs, but both showed much warmth and kindness. He just had to accept that this was how they were. He called his mother-in-law "Dearest Mum". There were times when both Lady Palmerston and indeed Minny herself thought Ashley was being rather priggish, but they bore with this.

Ashley for his part had to learn to live, like most people of strong convictions, in a less than perfect world. He could not cut himself off from people simply because he did not approve of everything they said or did.

There were many changes taking place in the life of the nation. In the same year as Ashley's marriage King George IV died and was replaced by King William IV.

A general election was held and Ashley, at worrying expense, was returned as Member for the town of Dorchester. The Government was now run by the Whig party. Consequently he lost his Tory job in the India Office and with it his salary. This was a blow to a young married man. It had proved a strangely hard fight to get his parliamentary seat for the Tories. The local Whigs in Dorchester, disappointed and enraged that their candidate did not get in, burned an effigy of Ashley on bonfire night instead of a guy! Ashley was finding out that politics could be very tough.

A greater change than a new government was in the air. For a long time moves had been made to try to alter the country's voting system. This was in order to obtain a fairer Parliament and involved the question of democracy, the form of government in which the will of all the people should have greater sway. This was not popular with the Tories, under the Duke of Wellington, who thought things should stay as they were and that the present form of government worked, on the whole, very well. Yet even the Duke, grumbling to himself, could see that the demand for a fairer voting system would not be quelled.

That ordinary people wanted a greater say in things became evident and agitators went further than just grumbling and muttering and causing a nuisance. Nottingham Castle was set on fire, Bristol prison was broken open and the Bishop's palace and the Mansion House were subject to arson attacks. It was very frightening. Mobs were at work here, trying to catch the attention of the Government. It became clear that a parliamentary bill would have to be brought in which would alter the distribution of parliamentary seats and make it possible for more ordinary people to vote. It was a strenuous struggle to get this Bill passed but at last, on 4th June, 1832, under the Whigs, the Bill became law. People lit bonfires all over the country, just as though a great war had ended. They felt they had achieved a great victory.

This law sorted out the numbers of Members of Parliament in different areas more fairly. It also gave the vote to all men of full age who owned or occupied a house worth £10 a year. It was to be a long time before the franchise, as voting was called, became all-embracing and even longer before the vote was given to women. But the Bill, known as the Great Reform Bill, did move the nation towards more democratic government and was a landmark in the British story. Of course, many Members lost their seats and not everyone was pleased.

For Ashley this was a formative time in his political and social thinking. He had made a friendship, conducted mainly by letter, with the poet Southey whose views much impressed him. Southey had become very angry on hearing of the cruelties inflicted on the climbing boys – the sweeps' apprentices – and had also become upset at what he had heard about the working conditions of the children of the poor. These were worlds that Ashley knew nothing about and he was intrigued and disturbed by what Southey wrote to him. Rather curiously, since Ashley was a conscientious MP, he did not know that a fellow MP, Tory Michael Sadler, had already introduced a Bill known as the Ten Hour Bill to limit the hours of children's work in the factories, nor that a select committee had been set up to report on the working conditions of factory children. Perhaps Ashley had been busy elsewhere. At any rate, he had known nothing of all this. He was to find that the cry of the distressed children was to pound in his ears more and more loudly and that he would never be able to get rid of this sound until their troubles were ended.

# 6

# THE BATTLES BEGIN

The next few years saw action time for Ashley. He was tested both as a Member of Parliament and as a Christian.

There was excitement for all Members of the Commons when a fire burned down the Chamber where they met. They then moved into the Court of Bequests, the home of the House of Lords, and the Lords moved for the time being to the Painted Chamber. The Commons remained in their temporary quarters until the new Chamber was built in 1852.

Unrest in the country persisted. Agitators were harshly punished and some Dorset agricultural workers received a sentence of transportation out of the country. They were known as the Tolpuddle Martyrs.

But life went on and for Ashley brought great personal joy. He became the father of a son, known quaintly in babyhood as Sir Babkins. Tiny Anthony was the first of what would be a large family.

Important issues took over Ashley's life. He began to be drawn into the lives of people far removed from his own social circle. He could not help being interested in the Chimney Sweeps Act brought in by some Members. This Act was passed in 1834 but he did not at that time realize how, within a few years, he himself would be involved in fighting a strenuous battle on behalf of the sweeps' apprentices, the "climbing boys".

His big chance to show what he was made of came when he was asked to take up the cause of the child factory workers. He was deeply shocked by reading the report that had been circulated about the dreadful conditions and long hours of working children. Ashley came from a typical land-owning family and had absolutely no knowledge at close hand of the populous northern towns and cities with their mills and factories and scramble for increased profits. Michael Sadler's report was a real chapter of horrors.

Britain's important textile industry, based on wool, had been transformed by the use of the steam-engine, giving greater power and reliability than the water wheel and giving freedom of movement to employers. Soon all aspects of textile manufacturing were taken from domestic workers in their homes and passed over to the new machines. This was not painless. It involved the recruitment of hordes of factory workers, including many children whose wages would of course be very small. And for these children life was hard. The hours were very long and the work caused permanent deformity in their limbs. Even the inventor Richard Arkwright admitted that the design of his machines had a bad affect on the children.

The boys and girls, known as "piecers", had to stand for hours in the worsted mills and make certain movements to assist at the moving machines. This involved lifting the left hand to grasp a machine-part high in the air, which raised one shoulder up, and at the same time the right knee bent inwards. When they had performed this action thousands of times, it was no wonder their bodies developed a lopsided stance and they could only limp along. They also had nasty accidents because there were then so few laws about covering dangerous machinery.

One overseer who gave information to Sadler's committee admitted that in a flax-spinning mill, where he had charge of nine little workers, six of them had peculiar feet and the other three had other deformed limbs.

Mothers and fathers did not usually want to

send their children to the mills but they were so poor they could not manage without the children's pathetic pay. Parents often cried when they had to shake their wretched children awake in the morning to get them to work on time.

The Commissioners who produced the report had an uncomfortable time as they began to uncover the horrible truth about the little workers. They visited the great northern industrial centres such as Leeds where they found several thousand children marching down the main streets wearing placards that declared: "The Ten Hours Bill." The procession swept relentlessly to the Town Hall to make its feelings known.

In Bradford the Commissioners visited one factory where, in the dinner break, they found themselves surrounded by children chanting a ditty they understood very well: "We will have the Ten Hours Bill; yes, we will, that we will . . ."

As the children danced wildly round, the Commissioners became quite nervous and retreated to the mill yard where they cowered until the children went back to work! The feelings of the operatives in Yorkshire and Lancashire were understandably very strong.

The children were not without champions in the north, sometimes quite ordinary people. Two men called Grant and Haworth forced their way into a meeting in Lord Palmerston's private apartments. They were determined to make him understand how heavy some of the work was for the children. He was not at first convinced. He was sure, he said, "the machinery did all the work". This made the men mad and they looked round for a way to demonstrate the truth to the noble Lord. They pulled two large chairs on castors together to represent the machinery and persuaded Palmerston and his servant to sit in the chairs. Then one man pretended to be the spinner and the other the child, the little "piecer". The two men then pushed the chairs up and down to show the movement of the machines.

"Stop, stop!" cried Palmerston at last. He could not believe that this represented the movement of the machines, but the men insisted it was so.

"This is just how it feels when you're pulling up the carriage," they declared. And they quickly rolled up their trousers to show their knobbly and deformed knees, out of shape from their early years in the factory.

"Pam" just had to be convinced and after

that he himself totally supported the cause of factory reform.

The full horror of the situation was brought home to Ashley. He was now approached by a Scottish MP and a north-country clergyman who urged him to take up the concern of the children – nobody else of the right calibre seemed to be available. It was not, frankly, a cause likely to shoot a parliamentarian to the forefront as a rising political star. Struggles had already begun to try to get the children's working hours made shorter in the Bill put forward by Michael Sadler, but this MP had lost his seat in the change of Parliament. Who could take his place? The consensus was that Ashley was the man – the only man – who could be the children's champion. Would he take on the job?

This was altogether unexpected to Ashley and he begged for a little time to think things over. He could appreciate that this would prove a time and energy consuming exercise. Anything that might affect industrial profits was a sensitive issue, for there were many important and powerful factory owners in the Commons. He went home and talked the idea over with Minny. As was his custom, he "spread the matter out before God" in prayer.

After this and getting Minny's wholehearted approval he knew he would – he must – say yes. "It seems no one else will undertake it, so I will," he said.

Minny encouraged him. "Go forward – and to victory!" she cried.

So Ashley said yes. He believed it was his duty. Like many of his actions, begun as duties, this one would lead to a consuming devotion. Ashley had heard the cry of the children . . .

There had been various attempts since the turn of the century to improve the lot of factory workers, especially the children. Workers of all ages felt aggrieved and that they were being exploited. In 1831, Sadler had brought in his Bill, called from then on the Ten Hours Bill. This would, he hoped, make it illegal to employ children under nine years of age, lessen the actual work of those aged between nine and eighteen to ten hours and two less on Saturdays and forbid night work to anyone under twenty-one. The existing punishing schedule of working hours was then quite common.

His Bill received a second reading and when asked to speak for the Select Committee, he produced the horrifying report that had so upset Ashley. Now that Sadler was out of Parliament, he could not go on with his Bill. So Ashley took it from there.

Even without travelling north to see things for himself, he found that he had tremendous support in the northern counties. There was much disturbance in the factory areas and some agitators were notorious for making strong, even wild speeches – such men as Richard Oastler, a powerful orator marked out by the Government as "dangerous". There were plenty of shocking stories to illustrate the plight of the little workers, stories for Ashley to pass on to Parliament. But he recognized that, in time of national recession after the Napoleonic wars, the factory owners were nervous that to give children shorter hours would result in less production and lower profits. Some of the work done by adults, it was said, depended on the help of the little workers. A spinner, they said, could not work without his little piecer, a weaver without his draw-boy.

Some mill owners, like John Fielden, the great master-spinner of Todmorden, were concerned about the children's welfare, but many did not really care and would persuade doctors to say that children were older than they really were or that the hours and hours of factory life were quite good for the children! The children were dubbed by one northern orator "little white slaves". The journalist and politician William Cobbett said sarcastically, "It has been decided that if the thirty thousand little factory girl children worked two hours a day less, our superiority in manufacturing would depart from us . . ." Indeed the House of Commons really believed this was so. Fortunes could not be made, it was said, or trade maintained without the long working hours of the children.

And all this, thought Ashley, in a so-called Christian country. Many of the children were paupers, sent to the mills from the workhouses where they had lived, with no parents or relatives to speak up for them. As Ashley found all this out and began to visit the North of England, where the mills and factories mainly were, and to meet some of the little victims for himself, he became more and more determined to fight for them and more and more dedicated to his task.

He took charge of the Ten Hours Bill from Michael Sadler and in February 1833 he told Parliament that he would bring in the Bill again. He got in some practice for this by talking to the London Society for the improvement of the Condition of Factory Children. Here he heard the welcome ring of applause and he impressed listeners by his speech. "I will not give any single moment on the question of the ten hours," he boldly asserted. He told his hearers that if his Bill was defeated, he would keep bringing it in until it did succeed.

He did not then realize that he would be doing this for the next fifteen years. Speaking to sympathizers in a Christian group was one thing, speaking to the tough Commons assembly was another. His intentions, though approved of by some Members of the House, alarmed others who were mill owners or had interests in the mills and who supported the Whig Government. Bringing in his Bill, Ashley spoke eloquently as he pleaded for the "slave children". But his appeal at this stage was based mainly on what he had heard and read. He had not yet seen enough at close hand to be able to present his beliefs with the passion and conviction that were crucial. The House moved to delay any further action and asked for a further enquiry, in the hope that this would take a long time and Ashley would forget about his Bill.

In spite of difficulties put in their way, those responsible brought out their report with amazing speed. Ashley urged them on. People were interviewed and children called to testify and everyone was forced to admit that the conditions were just as ghastly as had been suggested. Some improvements must surely be made. Yet there was no burning desire to make these improvements. And hardly anybody cared about the provision of simple education and moral teaching that Ashley wanted to see included. It was almost as though the children were little machines themselves, instead of small human beings.

Ashley became worried that time was passing and nothing getting done. He understood that Northerners were growing riotous about the long working hours and believed that revolution was on the cards. So he got in touch with Lord Althorpe and begged him to do something.

Lord Althorpe himself now produced a Bill. Sensing the feelings of the House, he gave his Bill certain limits but it did offer some improvements to children in the textile industry, though not to those in the silk mills. It was now agreed that children under nine years old should not work at all. Those between nine and thirteen should work eight hours. Some "education" should be given and inspectors should be appointed to see that things were correctly done.

Ashley was disappointed but felt that this Bill was better than nothing. He resolved to try again with an advanced Bill in the future. The lot of the children was still hard, but at least and at last they had a champion.

# 7.

# TENSE TIMES

Now Queen Victoria came to the throne. She was a fatherless girl of eighteen who had lived quietly, under quite strict supervision, with her mother in Kensington Palace. Her reign was to be great and glorious in many ways, but at the time of her accession total recovery had not been achieved after the Napoleonic wars. Apart from its aristocrats, Britain was largely a country of artisans, industrial labourers and agricultural workers and many were not happy with their lives. Unemployment was widespread and the standard of living low. Working people felt they needed greater power to alter things and some were incited to extreme measures.

Ashley continued steadily in his political career. He was also, as he approached forty, now well recognized as an important evangelical Christian and was much in demand as a speaker and as a president or chairman of church societies. He had made a friend called

Edward Bickerstaff, of similar views, who acted as support and counsellor.

Ashley held some views that were not universally accepted by all his acquaintances. And when he believed in something, he did so passionately. He had fervent hopes for what was described as The Second Coming. He believed Christ would soon come again on the earth, when the wrongs of the world that so worried Ashley would be severely sorted out and put right. He was rather upset that this had not yet happened. He was also very concerned that the Jewish people should return to Palestine. He did not envisage a Jewish sovereign state but a settlement of Jews, living as subjects of the Turkish empire, but under British protection.

On a more immediate level he was happy to be associated with various church organizations. He would allow his name to be put on official notepaper. This drew followers and subscribers and was good publicity for the organizations. These bodies included the British and Foreign Bible Society and the Church Pastoral Aid Society. This last organization, whose aim was to "increase working clergy and discreet laymen", caused something of a storm among those members of the Church of England known as High Anglicans. Ashley believed passionately in what he called the priesthood of the laity, by which he meant ordinary people, not ordained, who felt the call to carry out church work. He was rather critical of many clergy, whom he suspected of being lazy.

Ashley had now been married for about eight years and was blissfully happy with Minny and their growing family. Perhaps he still looked a little wistfully towards high political favour and poured out his feelings about this in his diary. He could sometimes feel aggrieved and easily snubbed – it was a weakness of his. But he was a happy man, despite his times of depression. Minny would sometimes get annoyed with him for becoming too involved in work or in religious battles of words. She did not think this at all necessary.

Through his aristocratic position, he came to know the new Queen socially. And Minny of course was the niece of the Prime Minister, Lord Melbourne. Ashley did not have a high opinion of the Queen's mental powers and spoke rather severely of her "small girlish mind". He perhaps overlooked her youth and inexperience. Yet within a few years he would be saying, "I cannot but love the Queen – she is so kind and good to me and mine". In her early years of rule Ashley rather mistrusted the influence of her Prime Minister, Lord Melbourne, a mature figure whose personality delighted Victoria and whom she looked upon as a kind of father.

But Ashley and Minny enjoyed their occasional visits to the palace and other residences of the Queen. These short stays were not wildly exciting but, as he said, "the civility of the servants and the comfort of the houses" were wonderful. He explained to friends that they had "mornings to themselves or rode through the park with Her Majesty". He spoke of her "kindness and condescension" and described the pattern of their visits. "10 o'clock for breakfast, 2 o'clock for luncheon. Ride or drive for two hours at 3, and 7.30 for dinner." A military band played during dinner and then they sat up until 11.30. Many visitors to the court thought the evenings with Queen Victoria excruciatingly dull but Ashley would have been too polite to put such thoughts into words.

He and Minny had a good time with their two eldest sons at Windsor Castle. The young Queen was fond of Minny, whom she described as "a nice amiable person", and thought the young mother looked lovely. And the boys were a great hit in their green velvet frocks – the normal outfit of small upper-class male children – and their long perfumed hair. The Queen was less fond of Ashley, whom she thought rather too enthusiastic about his projects, particularly his religious activities. He was also rather stiff in manner, she thought. They could both be obstinate characters.

She liked the company of young children and persuaded the little boys, Accy and Francis, to play ball with her in the long castle passages. Since these were lined with classical marble busts and important furniture, the boys were at first uneasy and "what would papa say" sprang to their lips. But being urged on by their hostess, they let themselves go and amid shrieks of laughter they relished sending the ball flying up and down the 500-foot long main corridor. This visit was a great success.

An unfortunate incident occurred when, after the fall of the Whig Government, it was suggested that the Queen should replace her Whig ladies-in-waiting with a rota of Tory ladies. The Queen was having none of this and told Sir Robert Peel so firmly. She was of the opinion that any such new ladies would be "household spies", introduced to spy on her movements. Anyway, they were not her personal friends. Sighing, Peel gave up the attempt to persuade her and to form a government. He had offered Ashley a post in the royal household, hoping for a good influence on the young Queen. But Ashley did not want this at all, he felt such a life would be a sort of prison and he was mightily relieved when the scheme fell through.

While the Queen was absorbed in matters of court etiquette, flashes of hostility appeared throughout the nation, more to the Government than to the Queen. What Ashley described as "the vast multitudes, ignorant and excitable", the working people of the day, were making their views felt. Some people banded together to form the Anti-Corn Law League. This rather mysterious title related to something very earthy and understandable – the desire of the people for cheap food.

During the recent wars, much land had been ploughed up so that more food could be produced. This land was poor and the corn grown on it was not good and could not compete in price with imported corn from other countries. So, with the coming of peace, it was decided to protect British agriculture. The Corn Laws of 1815 forbade the coming into the country of foreign grain, so long as the price in Britain was less than eighty shillings a quarter. This did not make things much better for the farming community and it meant that people could buy only British grain for bread-making and had to pay a high price for it. There was demand for these Corn Laws to be cancelled or "repealed" so that cheaper foreign grain could be brought in and cheaper loaves could be made and sold to hungry people. So the Anti-Corn Law League was formed with the slogan "Untax the bread of the poor!" A group of determined people wanted the old laws done away with and this group was growing. All this caused Ashley to shake his head. The land-owning constituency which he represented in Parliament was totally against getting rid of the Corn Laws.

In the same year as the founding of the League, Queen Victoria was crowned in Westminster Abbey. She wore a diamond circ-let on her head as she entered the Abbey and robes of crimson velvet with ermine fur, and later a gown of linen trimmed with lace. She had eight train-bearers, looking like a "cloud of silver".

There was a great contrast between the life-style of the Queen and aristocracy and that of the very poor who lived in squalor. The Queen had caught the message of instability in the country. She was much upset by a small Char-tist riot outside Buckingham Palace. Lamps were broken and a young hothead shouted out the French revolutionary slogan – *vive la République*! – then was promptly ashamed of himself and shook hands with the sentry. The royal family became agitated.

Who were these Chartists? Theirs was a movement for greater liberty and rights for the people and it arose out of discontent. They had thought that after the Great Reform Act of 1832 their lot would be easier but this had not happened. The cost of living was high and there was still much unemployment. They decided they needed greater political power to obtain real changes. Their leader was a fiery Irishman, Feargus O'Connor. Agitation turned to violence from place to place, with street fighting in South Wales and rick-burning in country areas. A Monster Petition was produced, a huge paper roll with various demands written on it, to which were put thousands of signatures. This petition was rolled up into a massive cylinder, four feet in diameter. It took twelve men to push it to the House of Commons, right up to the Speaker's chair. Alas the House of Commons refused to look at the petition. After this rebuff, there was further violence.

The aristocracy would have nothing to do with the Chartist movement. They were worried for their own safety and that of their property. Before the Chartist petition reached the House many noblemen had brought brawny tenants up from their country estates to stand by in their town houses in case of trouble. The Queen was advised to go away for a while and retreated to her country mansion, Osborne, in the Isle of Wight. The ruling classes were badly shaken by the Chartists.

It was altogether a worrying time for those in authority. A powerful orator in the North, a Wesleyan Minister called J. R. Stephens, addressed a great crowd about breaches of the Factory Acts. Speaking of employers who would not carry out the good provisions of the Acts, he gave a fierce warning.

"We will have everyone that dares to break the law sent to the treadmill; if that will not do we will have them sent to Botany Bay . . ." At this ringing speech the crowd cheered.

And that man of "reckless temper", Richard Oastler, had threatened to involve the children in acts of vandalism. He said he would teach them to put knitting needles into the machine spindles and so cause the machines to break down.

No wonder, when the government learned of all this, they shivered. The North had seemed a long, long way from Westminster, but now it seemed to be getting nearer all the time.

On a more cheerful level, a notable wedding took place. It was a national event which could not be ignored. It pleased some people but annoyed others. This was the wedding of the young Queen Victoria to her handsome prince, Albert of Saxe-Coburg-Gotha.

Many were delighted to see the Queen married. Officials thought her somewhat stubborn nature might be softened by a wise husband. Others were not too happy to have a German prince sitting beside their Queen and influencing her. It had to be recognized, though, that the Queen herself had German antecedents and German relatives. Sometimes German words or spelling affected her writing and pronunciation as when she was reported to be "schocked" at some action of Lord Palmerston, of whom she frequently disapproved.

The wedding was splendid, Victoria wearing a white satin gown trimmed with English Honiton lace. She wore a diamond necklace and the Prince's gift of a sapphire brooch. Her hair was wreathed in orange blossom. There were twelve train-bearers all in white and Prince Albert was tall and imposing in uniform. Trumpets sounded and the organ pealed out. The congregation admired the dignity of the small plump Queen. She later set off for Windsor with her "Dearest Albert".

Ashley was one of the few Tory Members of Parliament invited to the wedding. His relationship with the Prince was going to be variable. There were times when they would violently disagree, but on many important issues Ashley would find the Prince a great support. The Queen later became annoyed with Ashley because he would not support a motion to increase the Prince's civil list grant and make more money available to him. Ashley also disapproved of the royal yacht. He thought it was far too extravagant. There were times when the Queen was not pleased with Ashley at all.

Ashley and Minny and their eldest son Accy – short for Anthony – took a holiday to Scotland, which they loved. In fact, it was a holiday combined with business of a sort. They saw beautiful and impressive scenery and also features that were depressing and disturbing. They left the younger children – "the kids" as Ashley called them – with his sister and set off. Their journey was made partly by the new-fangled steam train of which Ashley was rather mistrustful – it went at twenty miles an hour! The remainder of the journey was by horse and carriage.

They came to a halt in the great city of Liverpool. Deciding to walk around, they were horrified by the swarms of dirty, ill-clad children wandering around. Minny lifted her dainty long skirts as even a few steps off the main streets into filthy alleys revealed nasty sights. There were open sewers and appalling smells.

The children mostly belonged to Irish labourers who, unemployed in their own country, had come to Liverpool to find work on the docks. Ashley and Minny were deeply shocked. Could this be the same England as the one in which they normally lived? Or even the same city as the fine Liverpool with its splendid public buildings through which they had just driven? It made them both shudder. They were discovering how the very poorest of the poor actually lived.

There were so many amazing inventions, apart from the steam railways, at which the British distinguished themselves. And if while on holiday they wished to write home to their relatives and friends, they could do so for the wonderful price of one penny, for the new Penny Post had just been introduced. This was most gratifying. But when the family reached home they found that Lord William Russell had been murdered in his bed by an unknown hand. Also there had been an assassination attempt upon the Queen herself, by a seventeen-year-old, a member of a secret society.

These were tense times indeed. As Ashley wrote, "Our system begets the vast and inflammable mass that lies waiting, day by day, for the spark to explode into mischief . . ."

# 8.

# UP THE CHIMNEY AND DOWN
# THE MINE

Ashley now took on in earnest two of the biggest fights of his life. One was quickly successful and ended years of the most shocking scandal. The other battle was to carry on for years and prove very exhausting. These were not fights with swords – though the age of duels was not yet over – but fights with words and policies. They were fights waged publicly on the floor of the House of Commons in speeches and privately in argument, discussion, research and a lot of prayer.

Ashley realized that people were not very idealistic and were most worried about the economic situation. To pilot a Bill through Parliament for the betterment of working conditions would prove a tough fight indeed. But he knew he had to take up these causes and he felt they were God-guided tasks.

To get himself ready for these battles in the House he set his researchers to bring him exact information. He mastered all his papers thoroughly so that he really knew what he was talking about and could answer the most piercing questions confidently. Ashley knew he was not a great orator and that some people considered his Christian emphasis eccentric, but he did not care about that. He knew that he must always be very practical if he was to convince anyone.

He now began a lifetime's campaign on behalf of the Sweeps' Apprentices, usually known as the climbing boys. An Act had been passed some years earlier to improve their lot but had been largely ignored. Although Ashley lived a long way from the factory children of the northern cities, neither he nor any of his grand friends were far away from the little sweep boys. Mostly unseen, these little boys lived a life of terror in the chimneys.

It so happened that early one morning Ashley glanced out of his window into the mews at the back of his London house. He saw a small boy limping along beside a large man. They were both covered from head to foot in soot and dressed in filthy rags. Ashley was struck with horror at the appearance of the child. The limbs of this little boy were all twisted, he dragged one leg along and he was bent over by the weight of a bundle of rods and brushes, the tools of the sweeper's trade. He was getting a good cuffing and cursing from his master.

Upset at the sight, Ashley went downstairs at once to look into the matter. What he discovered was more horrific than could be imagined. He knew vaguely that the job of the children was to haul themselves up the big chimneys above the grates where the coal fires – the common form of heating then – had been burning and to sweep down the soot. He had never realized all that this entailed. Like many people, he had never given it much thought.

He discovered first of all that the children had to be young and small to wriggle up the chimneys and try not to get wedged in. They were got ready for their nasty work by first being rubbed over with salt water in front of a hot fire, to harden the skin. This in itself was painful. The actual climbing job was horrible. Up in the dark chimney, with soot falling into their eyes and getting into their throats, and with the chimneys sometimes still quite hot, the experience was terrifying. Naturally the little boys hated all this and would struggle, only to be forced up farther by their masters. They were frequently beaten. Many of these pathetic little creatures were the illegitimate children of prostitutes, some were pauper children from the workhouses, some were even sold to the sweeps by desperately poor parents. The children were often seriously hurt, bruised, battered, scorched. Some even died.

Why had nobody become enraged about all this? Parliament had comforted itself by passing the earlier Act but things had slid back and the awful practices continued. Even the housewives of the land could not be excused from shame at their part in employing the child climbers. They were said to believe that the new-fangled machinery now brought in made more dirt in the rooms – not true – and that the boys were a better proposition. So they hardened their hearts and went on employing the unfortunate boys. Since the sweep arrived very early in the morning, they hardly ever saw the climbing boys at their work or heard the cries and sobs. It seemed that nobody cared about the boys.

But a champion was at hand! Ashley now began his long hard fight for their freedom. He took a very personal interest in this cause and he sought out the boy he had seen in the mews. After some bargaining, the sweep master was bought off and the little boy's father found. Ashley offered to educate the boy at his own expense and release him from a life of misery.

And so, because of Ashley, the boy left his life in the "soot-hell" and went to school, a lad who could hardly believe his good fortune. At the Union school in Norwood he did well and Ashley made sure that no climbing boys were ever employed in his own house.

Convincing Parliament and the general public of the need to tighten up the law was another matter. With the general tension of the times, the economic recession, a certain indolence on the part of the upper classes and worry about revolutionary activities, the concerns of one group of little boys was not a big issue for Parliament. Ashley did not see it like that and in his speeches to the House he tried to shake up his listeners' consciences about the ghastly life, sometimes very short, of the climbing boys.

Ashley's Climbing Boys' Bill became law in 1840 but it was to be many years before this dreadful scandal really died out. In fact, it would be another thirty years before there could be said to be real victory. As so often, something really terrible had to happen before the public was sufficiently ashamed. When a child called Christopher died after a chimney climb, Ashley wrote in his diary, "A death has given me power once more to appeal to the public."

He was finding these battles for the under-privileged very tiring. He suddenly realized that he now had compelling interests in so many good causes. He said, almost with a smile, "My hands are too full – Jews, chimney sweeps, factory children, church extensions, etc . . . yet we must persevere, there is hope."

All this took its toll. He suffered from indigestion, partly no doubt because of the irregular hours of the House and with delayed meal-times, and partly because he was a natural worrier. He also endured what he described as "roaring in the ears" which later generations would have recognized as tinnitus, an unpleasant sensation in the ears.

But when he left his duties behind and entered his comfortable home and shut the front door, he was able to relax. There was Minny running to him, always fresh and lovely, generally smiling, refusing to let the severe issues of Ashley's business life affect their home environment. And there were the children – all with their special nicknames – crowding round, eager to see him and tell him of their doings. They were not frightened of him as he had been of his father.

There were cuddles for the little ones and games with the older ones. And they saw the serious face relax, the blue eyes light up and then out came one of Ashley's famous jokes. Nothing made him feel so good as being with his family. Even when he had important thinking to do, he never minded the little ones crawling round his feet, or the shouts and laughter and rough humour of the older ones. He made sure that his home was filled with all the love and joy that had seldom come his way. Minny provided a serene, happy background and against this Ashley was content.

It was just as well that he had this stable home life, for national affairs were not improving. The trade depression was still there and the agitation to get rid of the hated Corn Laws persisted. Harvests at that time were generally poor and Britain had entered upon a decade that would be called later the Hungry Forties. There was much to worry about in the land.

Ashley's second big fight of the 1840s began after he became chairman of an investigation into working conditions for children in industries which had not been included in the Factory Act. First of all, Commissioners decided to look into conditions in the coal-mines. So they visited the mines, poked around, asked questions and made sketches. The drawings they had made created a dramatic impact among the general public. There had been an attempt in Parliament to stop the report and the drawings from reaching the public, but copies did get into the hands of Members and other influential people. What they read and saw put them off their breakfasts.

The Commissioners had discovered things they could scarcely believe. The sketches that accompanied the report told of a life that was dangerous, inhuman and often sexually abusive. The pictures showed girls and women, almost naked, bent double with chains round their waists, fastened to trucks underground. They crawled on their knees, dragging the coal up narrow passages, the roofs scarcely above their heads. There were girls working alongside naked men and little children living in a world of darkness. These tiny "trappers" had to sit in the dark and open and shut little trap doors – which ventilated the mine – to let the coal trucks through. Once the truck had gone by they were again in the dark, dirty silence, all by themselves in the blackness of the mine.

Other children worked ankle-deep in water at the pumps. Adolescent boys and girls, half-naked, clung together as they were brought up by a swinging rope from the depths below. The hours for children and adults were very long, seldom less than twelve at a time. Sometimes the children were employed as "enginemen" to let down and draw up the cages in which the miners went down to the coal face. Since the children were so young, they were sometimes distracted. Once a child of nine caught sight of a mouse and at the critical moment the rope slackened and the cage fell down causing an accident. Then it was the child who got into trouble. It was even said that a child of three was taken into the mine by its father and told to hold a candle.

The worst protected of the children were those from the workhouses – orphans and illegitimate children – who were employed in large numbers in Staffordshire, Lancashire and the West Riding of Yorkshire and bound by a contract for twelve years from the age of eight. If they refused to go to work they could be sent before a magistrate and even imprisoned. Not only were these working conditions horrendous but the qualities that Ashley cared so much about – education and spiritual training – were totally lacking. The mine bosses had no use for any of this and the mine-owners, mostly upper class men living far away, really did not think about or know anything of what went on underground. They cared mainly about the production of coal and their profits.

Ashley knew what he had to do. He himself went down 450 ft into a mine to see for himself. "I thought it a duty," he wrote. He said, emphasizing something he always believed: "It is always easier to talk if you have seen . . ."

He told the House he meant to introduce a Colliery Bill forbidding women and children from working in the mines. There was no great rush to support him; in fact, the usual attempts to frustrate him. A month after the Report had appeared, Ashley got up in the House to make the speech that would for ever alter things for the defenceless pit workers.

As he rose and stood at the table to begin his appeal, he felt a surge of encouragement as some words of Scripture came into his mind: "Only be strong and of a good courage." So he began his speech and as he spoke with passion his words really touched the hearts of his hearers. One or two were even in tears. He reminded them that not many years earlier the black slave trade had been stopped by the British. Now, he urged them, was the time to liberate "by a cheap and harmless vote" thousands of women and children who were themselves slaves and a disgrace to a Christian country.

When he had finished his speech there was a moment of silence, then cheering broke out.

Even people who did not usually share his views, or even like him very much, hurried up to pump his hand and clap him on the back. The Queen sent a warm message by Prince Albert. Ashley was praised in the press and, perhaps to his surprise, his Bill was passed with astonishing speed. He felt very thankful to God for the victory.

He also believed that if public conscience could be roused in this way, it might soon be possible to improve the lives of the factory workers, for whom the Ten Hours Bill was not perfect. He was very disappointed that, as yet, he could not get the House to pass laws enforcing some education and religious instruction for the little workers, which he thought could well be arranged by the employers. They seemed not yet ready for this.

Ashley had other problems. These related to the living conditions on his father's estate. Ashley knew that the workers lived in squalid housing and were badly paid. Often the estate farmers paid them "truck" – that is, in goods or provender or liquor – instead of the money they badly needed. It was most embarrassing for him since, so long as the land belonged to his father, the Sixth Earl, he could do nothing about it himself.

To make matters worse, a "women's liberationist" of the day, Harriet Martineau, taunted him publicly that while he was attacking conditions on estates and in factories in the North, his own family estates were worse. He was even branded a hypocrite which hurt him badly since he had no power to alter anything. At last he decided he must speak out and this he did in Dorset at a public dinner. He told his well-filled and prosperous hearers that they should live less luxuriously so that they could pay their workers better and give them healthier homes to live in.

This speech caused a mighty explosion of anger and Ashley realized that in Dorset he had become very unpopular. His father soon heard about the speech. He was a man with a quick temper and he ranted and raved at Ashley, declaring that farm labourers could easily live on six or seven shillings a week – though he admitted he did not know how. Once again father and son were at loggerheads and had an almighty row.

Ashley was in difficulties with both his father and his constituents. It was all very frustrating.

# 9.

# DECISION TIME

Ashley made some tours to keep in touch with what was actually going on. He set off with Minny and her brother William. They visited Manchester and the surrounding area, looking at mills and talking to owners and workers. He was impressed with the Ashworth mills where he saw "cleanliness quite astonishing" and noticed the good accommodation for the workers. Some of the mills he thought pretty dreadful.

Ashley was not very happy visiting the factory areas of the North. The energy of new ideas and new machinery seemed to him to produce a hectic pace of life not to his liking. But he forced himself to make these visits. Mill-owners generally did not care too much about their workers who were caught up in the boom and bust ups and downs in the cotton trade.

There was a wide gap between what Ashley saw as needful when he toured the North and what could be accomplished when he got back to Parliament. Sometimes the Northerners did not understand all the processes that had to be gone through and spoke harshly to Ashley, which was distressing when he was trying so hard to help them. But he congratulated them on their patience and lack of violence. Any open aggressiveness really upset him.

The North held many horrors for Ashley. Once, visiting in Manchester with two Inspectors, he listed the many unsavoury places he felt forced to pass through. In what he always called his "perambulations", he passed through "cellars, garrets, gin-palaces, beer-houses, brothels, gaming houses and other resorts of vice and violence". No one could say he was ignorant of the dark underworld of the very poor and the degraded.

As well as all this travelling and note-taking, Ashley had much work to do back in London. There was a grand railway boom and Ashley was made chairman of the parliamentary committee dealing with railway matters. He was rather hesitant about this, feeling quite unnerved by train travel which he thought dangerous. He thought it was a good idea to say a prayer before journeying on these new mighty monsters!

The word *hunger* stalked the politics of the mid-

1840s. It affected ordinary people, landowners, politicians – and Ashley. He found himself with one great problem that he had to resolve. It concerned getting rid of the hated Corn Laws which, to most of the population, meant the threat of famine. People believed that if the Corn Laws were abolished and they were allowed to bring cheap foreign grain into England, there could be cheap bread for all. This view grew and grew in the minds of everyone except those who were used to making profit from protected grain supplies in England.

Since Ashley was and had always stood as a Tory Member of Parliament, he was expected to go along with Tory Party views. These views were emphatically against repealing or getting rid of the Corn Laws. Secretly, some of the high Tory politicians, like the Prime Minister Sir Robert Peel, had come to the conclusion that they were going to have to alter the law to prevent a revolution. And in his own heart Ashley was coming round to this view also. He was very upset at what was happening in Ireland, where a great potato famine was already causing hunger in that troubled land.

He began to feel uncomfortable among his party members, for while he stood as their representative in Parliament he was expected to represent their Tory views. For some time he had been finding that he was not a convinced "party man", but one who looked mainly to the principle of individual issues and what was best for most people, rather than for his party.

Ashley was a most compassionate person who could easily sympathize with other people's troubles and the idea of people being hungry appalled him. He was particularly upset by the situation in Ireland. This troubled country, for historical reasons, was in a state of helpless hostility to England and had so many English troops on duty that the country was one big garrison. The Government was always nervous about Ireland.

People's conditions of life there depended largely upon their potato crop, which they grew on small pieces of land and which, with milk or buttermilk, largely formed their diet. A severe potato blight which had reached the country across the Atlantic was now attacking the crop. In England, people enjoyed potatoes as one among many vegetables but in Ireland the crop was a matter of life or death.

There was now bad news from Ireland. In Armagh there was hardly a sound potato to be found. Panic began. Famine soon became a dreadful reality. Nobody knew what to do – there was no knowledge in those days of protective spraying.

The Government in England grew daily more worried. It did its name no good to hear of starving people roaming through Ireland begging for food or of bitter demonstrations and signs of despair. Several very severe winters afflicted Ireland, with heavy snowfalls, and attempts to offset the distress was spasmodic and not very successful.

All this reached a desperate pitch within the next year or two and many people were forced to emigrate. Landlords went to British North America and great numbers of poor Irish came to England.

It was obvious that something had to be done. Ashley was much disturbed and, as usual, practical. He brought matters home to his own hearth, insisting that no potatoes should be eaten by his family during this terrible time and himself held a collecting box for the hungry in the streets of Mayfair. A National Fast Day was held and Ashley was stern with himself, taking only a mug of cocoa and some dry bread.

At last the Prime Minister seized the nettle and made his decision. The Corn Laws must go. He himself endured much unpleasantness, occasioning harsh words and waving fists from his former friends and sometimes being bludgeoned into silence when he tried to speak in the House. But he stood firm. He had been urged to produce the necessary political action by Lord John Russell, the Whig leader. "Good old Johnny!" said Ashley.

So, in the spring of 1846, the hated Corn Laws were got rid of, in one of the most memorable sessions in the history of Parliament. Ashley had finally supported the decision to repeal the Corn Laws but he now had personal problems. He had written an open letter to his constituents trying to explain the change in his attitude. It is always difficult for politicians to change their views and his behaviour did not go down well. He now found he was unpopular on all fronts.

He said, "The Corn Law League hate me as an aristocrat; the landowners as a radical; the wealthy of all opinions as a mover of inconvenient principles." He went on, perhaps with wry humour, to list others who had no opinion of him. Perhaps he exaggerated but he was certainly nobody's favourite at that moment. Many unkind things were muttered about him.

He knew he had to make a personal decision and this he now did. He decided the only gentlemanly thing to do was to resign his parliamentary seat and he took the necessary steps. It was a big decision and did not come easily. He confided to his diary: "I shall resign my seat and throw up all my beloved prospects . . . God's will be done."

Ashley believed that this was the end of his parliamentary ambition. He was not now likely to be called to high office, perhaps even to become Prime Minister, as had once seemed possible. But with Christian grace he bowed to the inevitable and made the necessary arrangements to be released from his seat in the House. Leaving Parliament in this way was known as Applying for the Chiltern Hundreds.

Some of his recent achievements had given him satisfaction. His two great Lunacy Acts became law and ensured better care and hope for the mentally sick. He never lost compassion for these unfortunate people. He urged that mentally ill people should not be confined in private houses where it was impossible to inspect the conditions. He pleaded for more institutions to be built in Wales so that at least the poor sufferers could speak to someone in their own language. He again stressed the desirability of treating the mentally sick as ill people, to be dealt with in a respectful way and not despised or jeered at.

Before leaving the House he tried once more to introduce his Factory Workers Bill – the Ten Hours Bill. Maybe the House groaned as yet again he got up with his familiar plea. But he was not to be put off. "If you won't give us all we ask for, at least make some concessions," he begged. He managed to get improvements for the calico workers. But he could now do no more. Sadly he packed his personal belongings, left the House and went home.

# 10.

# OUT OF OFFICE

What on earth would Ashley do now? Minny might well have expected a spate of drama with Ashley brooding over his enforced absence from Parliament and being plunged into gloom. He had sat in the Commons for almost twenty years and really believed that he could do little for people if he were not a Member of Parliament.

To his surprise he quickly found that this was not so. His time out of office proved to be a kind of liberation. He could now make his own timetable, plan his own activities and enjoy to a greater extent the company of his much-loved wife and such children as were at home.

Accy, his eldest son, was boarding at Rugby School, and Francis, his second, had followed Ashley to Harrow. Accy was rather a worry to his parents. He tended to be idle and easy-going and not to take very readily to his father's religious advice. He was not a bad boy, but

Ashley sometimes felt a pang of anxiety when he thought of Accy eventually shouldering the responsibility for the family estates. On the other hand, Francis was all that his parents could have wished, a boy of natural Christian commitment but not unduly pious, a clever, happy lad whose future seemed very bright.

The younger children, boys and girls, were a constant delight to Ashley and Minny. There was nothing the parents enjoyed so much as taking their tribe on an outing – say to the Zoological Society's menagerie at Regent's Park. In his personal life, though worries did come, Ashley was content. His relations with his parents at St Giles were, unfortunately, little improved.

He now found that his days filled up quickly with appeals from various charities and church organizations and people with needs. Some had decided he was rich and looked for donations. This brought a sigh to Ashley who was not really wealthy, despite his comfortable lifestyle.

He realized many people thought that because he was an aristocrat and lived in large houses he must have loads of money to give away. Ashley had not yet inherited the family estates, and the allowance he received from his father was inadequate for the maintenance of his large family. There were so many things Ashley would like to have done that were at that moment quite impossible.

He decided, like politicians before and after him, to go on a major fact-finding tour. He felt that he must know much more of the conditions particularly of the poor city dwellers if he was to continue to be useful and to speak purposefully for them. He invited to go with with him Dr Southwood Smith, a friend with a great conscience about public health matters, as well as several London City Missioners whose work Ashley admired. Together they scoured all parts of London behind the grand public façades.

They received some horrible shocks. Up and down squalid courts and alleys they tramped, their good shoes squelching over insanitary cobbled streets, overflowing drains, uncleaned pavements. Everywhere seemed to smell horrible and Ashley noted few signs of pride or hope.

And all over the place small, dirty, shoeless children were crawling or climbing, looking as though they had never been washed since birth. Most were dressed in rags. There were hordes of slightly older ones who had no proper homes. These lived on the streets, by their wits. They would run down to the banks of the River Thames at low water and scrabble for coal, sticks, cork, anything that might be called treasure-trove and that they could use or sell. They were known when they did this as "mud-larks".

Adults they saw in the alleys were not much better clothed. All this made Ashley shudder but he marched on. He noted that in spite of their dreary surroundings, most of the children had bright faces beneath the dirt and if challenged would give him a sparky reply. They were never frightened of him.

The children did not know who Ashley was – the tall gentleman dressed in good dark clothes and with sidewhiskers in the manner of the day. It was soon whispered among the adults that this was the famous Lord who cared for poor people and did not despise them or wish them ill. No one ever turned on him with an insult or oath or demanded to know what he was doing there. For by now, most people had heard of him and realized that he was "different" from many of the politicians others had elected, and that he did mean what he said and he did care about them.

In spite of his fastidious upbringing and mannerly lifestyle, Ashley did not care how messy the children were – he would always stop and talk to any runny-nosed urchin. And in his fine mind he stored away all that he had seen for future reference.

Seeing so many mean streets and deprived people did affect Ashley's spirits and made him rather serious. He found himself critical of the lifestyle of many of his friends. After staying with royalty he wrote, ''The amount of waste in all things is prodigious . . .'' And after going out to dinner with some aristocratic friends he was forced to conclude, ''The very crumbs and scrapings of finished dishes in a thousand well-filled families would, week by week, sustain a hundred families.''

The more he saw of the way the poor lived, the more he was apt to make comparisons. For now he knew so much more of what deprived people really endured.

As well as poking round in London, Ashley went on a tour of inspection of factory districts. The North of England, its industry and special way of life were a mystery to Ashley – but one that he was more and more to penetrate.

He never found it easy to get on with Northern businessmen, mill owners, factory owners, coal-mine owners. Their lives and expectations were so different from his own as a landowning aristocrat. He thought that life in their big cities was ''all hurry and rush'' and the outspoken blunt speeches, often with overtones of violence, were hard for him to accept.

Yet he did respect and admire men of the character of John Fielden and, in spite of his being one of the most quarrelsome and awkward men in England, Richard Oastler, a Yorkshire land agent, a man of fiery temperament and provocative words but total devotion. Ashley recognized that for all workers, children and adults, living conditions were often so bad that people easily became inflamed and intemperate in their political approaches. This always upset Ashley. Although he could himself be most impassioned in his causes, he always strove for a reasonable, calm presentation and was greatly alarmed at the prospect of wild demonstrations and the vision of trade unions horrified him. He was a prisoner of his own personal history in many ways.

However, his industrial visits gave him plenty of facts and figures so that he was well armed when people flung questions at him. He was now better equipped to deal with problems.

He could not easily forget his parliamentary life and was constantly haunting the lobbies of the House of Commons, to meet friends and find out what was happening. He could hardly believe that he had now no proper place there. Soon, though, he became absorbed in a new interest that would continue throughout his life.

He was reading his newspaper one day when he noticed that someone was asking for helpers as teachers in a "Ragged School" in an infamously rough area of the City of London. Intrigued, Ashley wrote off for particulars. He was at once invited to visit one of these schools. This turned out to be in one room of a miserable building in an area thought dangerous even by the police.

Yet what he saw lifted his heart. A group of the dirtiest, worst-clothed urchins he had yet seen were learning to read. The odour in the room was unpleasant, the manners and habits of the children fairly disgusting. It seemed that many had fleas which they passed on to the teachers. Yet a sort of concentration had been achieved and there was an air of purpose in the room.

This was one of the new "Ragged Schools" that had recently been set up largely by four ordinary men – a London City Missioner, a clerk, a woollen-draper and a second-hand dealer. They were in the world's eyes four nobodies but they had seen a need and had done something about it. They called their project a "Ragged school" not to insult the pupils, but to make it clear to the children of the slums that it did not matter at all how poor they were or how badly they were dressed or whether they had shoes or not. They were all welcome. No normal school of the day – and this was before compulsory education – would have accepted these children. Even churches would have thought twice about inviting such scruffy little creatures into their premises. Hence the name Ragged Schools. Everyone knew where they stood.

In these schools there was an attempt to encourage a rough level of cleanliness and tidiness. But the teachers, mostly men and women from good homes, mostly Christian people, understood how and where the children lived. These boys and girls often had no proper homes at all; many were orphans and lived anywhere they could find a dry space. They tucked themselves in at night under arches, in sheds, under carts. One boy said he slept inside the great iron grass roller in Regent's Park, after climbing the railings.

These children would today be called streetwise. They had no normal happy childhood but were entirely occupied with getting food and keeping themselves alive. They were often sly, unreliable, devious. Innocent, sweet children they were not. Yet, once attracted to the Ragged School, a surprising number found that they could learn and liked to learn, though their syllabus was simple – reading, perhaps a little writing, learning from the Bible.

Above all, they grasped that someone cared about them, a novel experience, and in this atmosphere they bloomed. Of course things were not always perfect. There were times of bear-garden behaviour, with teachers taunted, windows broken, fights breaking out. These children had no sense of discipline. Yet within the walls of the Ragged School, they were conscious of a caring which was not dependent on their behaviour.

Within a few years eighty-two Ragged Schools had been set up and more than 8,000 pupils drawn inside. Ashley was delighted by the schools and threw himself into their support. He believed that, with God's blessing, the children could then become good-living citizens of the British Empire. A Ragged Schools union was formed and he soon became President. Of all the interests and charities he supported, his schools were probably among his best loved.

He was glad that he now had the time to

support the schools. He chaired meetings, gave advice, talked simply to the boys and girls and also collected money. His sense of humour was tickled as he stood in the lobby of the House of Commons, though himself out of office, and collected for the children whilst his former colleagues bustled by importantly with their sheaves of papers. No doubt he rattled his collecting tin loudly, not allowing Members to get by without making a contribution.

Later, after visiting Field Lane Ragged School, Ashley wrote, "I never go there without seeing something for which to thank God."

So for a little over a year Ashley turned from being a politician to being a philanthropist – one who does good to his fellow-creatures. This was not likely to give him a place in the annals of great statesmen, but in the book of life he was making a mark that many poor and underprivileged people would note.

The one big irony of his time out of Parliament concerned his everlasting struggle with the Factory Bill – the Ten Hours Bill. This Bill, over which he had wrestled for so many years, and which he had handed over to Member of Parliament John Fielden, was now passed in 1847. Ashley would certainly have liked to be the one to achieve this. However, he accepted that the main thing was the successful outcome of his long campaign for a better life for the children. The boys and girls would now work, if work they must, for shorter hours and, hopefully, be given some smattering of education. All this made Ashley a much happier man.

## 11.

# BACK IN THE COMMONS

In the summer of 1847 a General Election was held. Ashley had been away from Parliament for two sessions. He had had a very busy time and, somewhat to his surprise, found his charitable activities most enjoyable. He wrote that he was "almost willing to retire from public life". He reflected on the demands of parliamentary life – "the immense consumption of time . . . the constant demand on moral and physical energy . . . the enormous effort required to do the smallest good." He also said, somewhat cynically, that he had found "the total impossibility of reposing entire confidence in any public man". He had found many disappointments in his public life.

Yet he knew that he did love the House and that that was where the power lay to do public good. He thought it unwise to try to get back his old seat in Dorset, for he knew he had many enemies there. He was now offered the constituency of the city of Bath and to his delight won the seat. Violence had been expected at the hustings; these were unstable times. Ashley was mobbed one Saturday evening as he went to address a meeting and he was struck by an excited man but no harm was done. The meetings were hot and crowded but at the end of his major speech people cried, "Ashley for ever!" Even if not true, this was encouraging. He was able to write, "I am returned to Parliament in a singularly and unusually honourable way." He was back in the House.

He knew that he could not have many more years to sit in this House since his father was growing old. It could not be long before, taking on the Earldom from his father, he would sit in the Upper House, the House of Lords. So he must make the most of the opportunities of power he now possessed.

Once more Ashley was aware of being very hard up. The election expenses were always a problem though he had gone in for no extravagant advertising gimmicks. "I did not pay a single farthing; I had not an inch of ribbon, a banner, music or a procession," he said. The voters had to take him on his reputation. His insufficient income was always harassing him. He now had a large family and their wants were considerable. Anthony, his eldest son, was always an anxiety and had got into debt at school at Rugby. Ashley and Minny decided it was best for the boy to be sent to sea. This was in the hope that the open-air life and strict discipline would improve what was seen as a lax and unsatisfactory temperament.

The poor health of the family also worried the parents. The children were much loved and well cared for. But, at a time when little was understood about health care, hardly one of the children was truly healthy. Maurice, one of their sons, was now found to be epileptic and must live abroad in a warm climate. "He has become as languid as a drooping flower," wrote Ashley sadly. The little girls, Vea, Conty and Mary, were not robust and baby Cecil was sickly.

All this was naturally a worry to Ashley, on top of the many business approaches made to him as a man of conscience and influence. People were always wanting help and hoping for things to be done for them. Sometimes he felt depressed. Fortunately, he wrote out much of his worst depression in his diary but he often had black moods and it was left to Minny, with her happy and open disposition, to chase these moods away. Life was not always easy for her.

Hints of revolution rumbled like thunder on the national scene. This was a year of financial crisis, not only for Ashley but for the whole country. The state of the money centre known as "the City" was said to be disastrous. And there were continuing problems with Ireland, on the brink of starvation. Lord Clarendon told Lord Russell, "A great social revolution is going on in Ireland, the accumulated evils of misgovernment and mismanagement now coming to a crisis."

Ashley described the situation as "terrible, terrible, terrible!" and held a collecting plate in one of London's smartest streets. He observed, "Sad to see how many well-dressed people pass by and give not a brass farthing!" No wonder the Government were fidgety.

Ashley thought up one good notion that did work out. It gave him pleasure and encouragement and proved a good deal for hundreds of children.

He had heard that the colonies of Great Britain needed more people and more workers. These vast, comparatively empty lands, their development still in infancy, required more colonists to go and settle down in their new homes. It occurred to Ashley that many of the bright-eyed, lively boys and girls he met in the Ragged Schools might go some way towards meeting these needs. The young people could be directed into useful service in a new country and become a valuable asset. If given jobs and pay they would be less likely to get into trouble. And in the great open spaces of these new lands there was the prospect of good health.

Ashley became quite excited at this idea and did his utmost to promote it. At first he was able to get some money from the Government, persuading them to share his enthusiasm. After a while they refused to give any more so he set about collecting cash from private sources – from rich friends and acquaintances.

The young people were not forced to emigrate. But as many of them had no parents or families and no future in England, they were excited at the prospect they were offered. Whenever he could, Ashley would go down to the docks to say goodbye and see the young adventurers off on their voyage. He was impressed by the well-scrubbed boys in the rough but decent new suits provided for them.

There was a bit of unsureness at this stage – it was all a big step for the boys to take. Ashley encouraged them, pressed them to look for the best in their new opportunities and urged them, "Never forget to say your prayers." There he was sincere for he himself was in the habit of "spreading everything out before God" in prayer. And as the great ship slid down the gangway he prayed for the boys and their future. He felt somewhat like a great father to them. Didn't he understand boys? He had six of his own!

As time passed he was often delighted to hear of one and another having done well and made good. He was thrilled to learn of one boy quickly getting employment as a shepherd, strangely for a former town lad. And a girl called Caroline married her master's son and became quite a personality.

Ashley was delighted with all this news. The emigration scheme, he believed, was a useful enterprise on behalf of young people who otherwise had hardly any future except staying in England and getting into trouble and ending up in punishment.

Ashley still gave time to the Ragged Schools and his interest was taken up by journalists who wrote about it and brought the cause to other influential people. He was also able to give help right on the political doorstep. A City Missioner, a church worker, found a very bad slum near the walls of the new Houses of Parliament. Normally, Members of the House would not see any of this as they went home in their carriages or walked to their West End clubs. Ashley got to hear from the missionary, a man called Walker, of his struggle and of the resistance he was meeting in trying to bring the Good News of the Gospel to the miserable wretches who were packed together in this slum. It had become quite dangerous for Mr Walker and he had nowhere to work from. At last he found an old stable which, cleaned up, would make a useful base for starting a Ragged School.

When Ashley heard about this he first went, as was his custom, to see for himself. Convinced then that Walker must have the money to buy the stable, he made another collection among the Members of Parliament and passed the cash on to the missionary. "Now get on with it," he seemed to be saying. A school was soon started and good results followed. Once again, the name of Ashley had brought success.

Before going back to the Commons, Ashley and Minny had a holiday in his beloved Scotland so that he would be well and fit for the new session of Parliament. In spite of being separated from his children, which he hated, Ashley really enjoyed this break and was in the best of humour. He was not keen on the Lowlands, but loved the heights which he described as "bracing, with life-giving breezes." He said jokingly, "One's old limbs become elastic," though he was not so old, about forty-six. He enjoyed long walks, often in the Scottish rain, and was thrilled at the sight of the autumn colours in the Highlands. He thought it was as though a mighty giant, intent on painting a huge landscape, had spread out all the colours of his palette.

Moving from one aristocratic home to another he met many friends. He enjoyed a chat with the "dear old Duchess of Beaufort" and with "dear old Sir David Brewster" who, thought Ashley, "combined beautifully science and religion" – something Ashley was very interested in. Visiting one mansion Ashley revealed himself to be very much a man of his age in the matter of women's liberation. He was introduced to an authoress Miss Strickland and before he had even met her he feared that she would be a "blue-stocking", as intellectual women were then called. To his relief, Miss Strickland turned out to be a "good-natured, kind-hearted woman".

The idea of a working woman was obviously something beyond Ashley's comprehension. He did not think they should have a place in public life at all, with a few exceptions, like Elizabeth Fry, the prison reformer, whom he was forced to admire. He wrote down very plainly his expectations of the role of a wife and mother, which he found, mercifully, in his beloved Minny.

"The high and holy duties assigned to women by the decrees of Providence are essentially of a secret or retiring nature," he wrote "It is in the privacy of the closet that the soft yet sterling wisdom of the Christian mother stamps her impressions on the youthful heart."

In November the Queen opened the new session of Parliament and for the first time it was possible for her speech to be transmitted to the country's main cities by the new "electric telegraph".

Ashley could not say much to John Fielden in the House by way of congratulation on the passing of the Factory Bill, since Fielden had now lost his parliamentary seat. But everyone knew how relieved Ashley was over the success of the Bill for which he had fought for so long. He was not to know that the fight was not yet over and that the opponents of the Bill were still finding ways of getting round it.

So Ashley's parliamentary life had begun again. But he could not abandon the causes which had absorbed him during his time away from the House. He enjoyed a very varied life. During the following few months he dined with the Queen at Windsor, and attended a meeting of the Lambeth Ragged School where he saw "three-hundred and seventy children, decent, orderly, happy".

And in the House he was on his feet again. He spoke up in support of a Bill to allow Jewish Members of Parliament. Ashley was back in harness.

# 12.

# ALARMS AND EXPLOSIONS!

The spirit of revolution was now let loose in Europe, often in violence. As Ashley, far-sighted in foreign affairs, had warned: "Events are coming to the surface – we see a stir on the waves and we shall soon see the mass thrown up by the volcanoes . . ." He was right. The year 1848 proved this.

A republic was declared in France, with the king escaping to England. Austria was crumbling to pieces. Italy was in open revolt. Berlin was troubled with riots in favour of a new constitution.

Things looked grave for England. Here there was still high unemployment, falling revenues, serious disagreements within the church; and sometimes, where groups were still active, revolutionary threats in Britain, orchestrated from afar. The poet Shelley, when exiled in Italy, had long ago in one of his poems called on the men of England to rise and destroy the rich governing class which, he believed, exploited and plundered them. For the Government and many of the people this was an era of fear. Ashley was sworn in as a special constable.

Mercifully, England suffered least of all and escaped full-blooded revolution. Ashley was of the opinion that the Christian faith, however poorly expressed, contributed to a valuable steadiness. He believed that the work of the City Missionaries in the slums and the faithful witness of the parish clergy had held back the breakdown of society. Even the Secretary of State for the Home Office confessed that the behaviour of most people in the big cities testified to the on-going evangelical work among the underprivileged – the people most likely to want to express their despair in riots. These were certainly difficult times when the nation had every reason to be afraid.

The second fear that swept the country was that of plague. The dread disease of cholera had reached England. It was often fatal. People did not understand that the disease was produced by germs carried in contaminated water. They had never even heard of germs and thought that infected air had something to do with the illness. Had they but known it, the conditions for the spread of cholera were all around them.

Ashley was deeply interested in public health matters and for some years had been agitating on this theme – mostly to deaf ears. He now had a chance to do something practical. He was invited to become a Commissioner on a new Board of Health. He was on holiday when he received the letter making this request and at first his heart sank. He knew this job would bring "trouble, anxiety, reproach, abuse, unpopularity" but reflected, "How could I refuse?" So he took on another large fight in which he would achieve only partial success. Nothing was clear cut in these parliamentary battles.

Public health was then curiously known by the unromantic name of Sanitary reform. It was certainly an unromantic subject. The increasing population of the country and the huddling together of so many people in large towns and cities had brought special problems. These mainly concerned the quality of the water, particularly in the capital city, as well as the drainage of the city and also the cemeteries. There were still open sewers. When these were flushed, as they had to be, many were emptied into the River Thames, London's main water supply. It is not hard to imagine the nasty quality of this water, some of which would be drunk. The cemeteries were also terrible sources of infection.

There was no general group of people whose job it was to get these matters right. The immense ignorance of health matters did not help.

When Ashley agreed to take on his new job on the Health Board he found he was to work with another Commissioner, Edwin Chadwick, a well-known public figure. He was not going to find this easy. In fact he never found it easy to work on equal terms with other people. From his lofty height as an aristocrat and a Member of Parliament and a tall, impressive-looking man, he was accustomed to giving orders and making decisions. He was good at talking to people on a lower social level without seeming to patronize them. But working with equals found him at his most uneasy. And Chadwick was known as an awkward person to work with. However, these things had to be done and the Commissioners began their task.

They went about their work with a will. They ordered inspections of buildings and suspiciously dirty outhouses. They enforced cleaning and lime-washing and the destruction of germ-breeding rubbish. The Board fought hard to obtain better drainage, on a mains system, and to improve burial facilities. It was an uphill struggle; at every turn someone raised objections, be they landlords or undertakers. Ashley was sometimes near despair.

The existence of the Health Board continued for six years after which it closed down. Ashley was greatly upset at this and brooded about the future of the country's health. It was to be some time before different measures improved the nation's physical wellbeing. Ashley pondered on what he had really accomplished. Some insanitary areas had been cleaned up and some good schemes for better drainage and water supply had been set in motion. Meantime, the fearful cholera, in later years to be eradicated from Britain, was taking its deadly toll. The epidemic carried off 58,000 lives. But for the diligent work of the Health Board, this total might well have risen much higher.

Whatever had or had not been accomplished, Ashley had impressed his Christian belief on those around him. This was that there was a huge connection between religion and social conscience. He was convinced that people's living conditions had a great affect on their behaviour and that it was hard for people to live good lives when everything around them was degrading.

This was a novel idea then for people to grasp. Ashley pointed out that Christian people, if truly dedicated, must get involved not only in speaking about Christ and offering Him to the masses in church services or in halls, but must also give attention to such matters as drains, overcrowded living conditions, infection, rubbish clearance, etc., etc. This was a new and not altogether popular view, particularly among the upper-class evangelicals among whom Ashley lived and moved. But he held doggedly to these principles.

He told a group of young men at a meeting he was chairing: "Christianity is essentially practical."

A third fear attacked Ashley personally. This was for the health of his family and particularly for his beloved second son, Francis. Ashley himself managed to escape cholera even though he had stayed in London where the plague had been rampant. Though not so robust as he had been and needing to walk with a stick, he was reasonably well and had carried on throughout the epidemic. But he had worried constantly about his children.

His anxiety over Francis had nothing to do with the cholera outbreak. This was a case of pleurisy, an illness which afflicted Francis while at his school, Harrow. Parents were perpetually fearful over their children's health for so much ignorance persisted on these matters.

Ashley and Minny now received an urgent message to go to Harrow and they hurried off. So-called cures were primitive and there were none of the drugs that would have been available in later times to help the invalids. Francis was seriously ill but smiled at seeing his parents. As well as being a true joy to them, he was popular with his schoolmates and the pupils moved around very quietly when they knew he lay ill.

Ashley realized that Francis knew he might not recover but was not afraid at the thought of death. He had received early in life from his father the assurance of God's love and of forgiveness and acceptance in Christ. A naturally religious young man, Francis now knew a true peace of mind. Ashley read to him from the Bible and talked quietly and simply to his son. There were private moments when Francis found the strength to pay tribute to the lead given by his father to the knowledge of God's grace.

Ashley was deeply moved. Not long after this Francis took a turn for the worse and died. He was buried at Harrow and his schoolfellows attended his funeral.

For a while Ashley and Minny were distraught. This was a son they had so much relied on and in whose future they had had so much confidence. But they were comforted by the strength and idealism of that young life, even as a schoolboy. Ashley and Minny believed that Francis was now "enjoying the blessed presence of his Maker". In their simple evangelical faith, they had no fears for him.

An extraordinary event now took place that would cause much head-shaking among those of Ashley's acquaintances who thought him eccentric. It was certainly bizarre. It arose from his friendship with a London City Missioner named Tom Jackson.

This man exercised a unique ministry among London criminals and was known and trusted among a motley crowd of pickpockets and other crooks whom he tried to help to a better way of life. Through Jackson, Ashley met and talked long to a discharged criminal. They had a chat about the emigration scheme which Ashley had organized for the street children of London. Ashley asked the man if he would want to emigrate if he had the chance.

"I should jump at it!" was the quick reply. Ashley spoke to Tom Jackson about it and shortly after this he received a letter written to him from forty discharged convicts, a sort of "round robin". This pleaded with him to come and talk to them.

So on a lovely summer night he left his civilized surroundings and made his way to London's East End. Here he was confronted by an amazing sight – an audience of 400 criminals who had come specially to hear him. Some were roughly dressed, some gave the appearance of having money. Ashley, having said a prayer, was greeted with reverent silence. He spoke very straightly and wanted to know the nature of the men's former crimes.

At a word from Tom Jackson, whom they plainly trusted, the men divided themselves into groups – petty criminals on one side, those who confessed to more serious crimes on the other. Despite Ashley's unmistakably upper-class appearance, the men responded easily to him and several got up to speak. They made it clear that, for many of them, desperate as they were, crime had seemed the only way to make a living and get food for their families. "We must either steal or die," one declared. Jackson urged them to pray but one spoke for many when he answered, "Prayer is good but it won't fill an empty stomach!"

The point of the men coming together and asking for Ashley to be there was that they wished to emigrate and start a new life in some younger country. There they felt their past could be left behind and they might have opportunities for more honest living, and be less likely to end up in prison.

They all looked so keenly at Ashley. Once again he must take upon his heart the burdens of others. How could he refuse to help? He was deeply touched when one man asked simply, "Will you ever meet us again?" Perhaps "do-gooders" had come to them before with big speeches and religious platitudes and had done nothing; now they were dealing with a man of integrity whose word was his bond.

After promising to return whenever they called for him, Ashley left, his head buzzing. As usual he wasted no time in getting on with things. Money to support such a scheme was obviously the first item and Ashley contacted a wealthy banker acquaintance. Lo and behold, all problems were soon settled. Arrangements were quickly made and within three months a dozen men had left for Canada to a new life. A year later another 300 left to begin new, stable lives without the temptation to turn to crime.

Ashley's "thieves' meeting" was an event that turned out very well. Alarms and explosions were not the only features of Europe's revolutionary year – not in England, anyway.

# 13.

# CHANGES

In 1851 an exciting event took place in the life of the nation and something important occurred in Ashley's personal life.

England was thrilled and to some extent revived by the setting up of the Great Exhibition. This was the idea of the Queen's husband, the Prince Consort – a man of culture. He had the vision of a huge exhibition, a tribute to art and commerce on an international scale. This was to be held among the lawns and flowers in Hyde Park, in a remarkable building. It consisted of domes of glass caught in a web of slender cast-iron. It was known as the Crystal Palace because it shone blindingly in the sunshine. It was designed by the famous Joseph Paxton.

The theme of the exhibition was Peace and Prosperity. All nations contributed to the exhibition but it was to do England much good.

A lot of argument preceded the completion of the exhibition, but the opening day came at last in May when the Queen of England, so proud of her husband's idea, drove to the site in her carriage. She wore a fine crinoline and a famous flashing diamond. She loved the hum of life that she felt around her.

The people loved the exhibition and it made a huge profit. Among the exhibits were machines, furniture, textiles. Huge choirs sang. It was all a sign that Britain was entering upon more peaceful and prosperous times. Revolutionary ideas seemed to have been dampened down. Britain now led the world in commerce and manufacture and society seemed more harmonious. Every mill and factory was busy and had plenty of work. The Exhibition seemed a symbol of all this. The historian Macaulay wrote of those days as "a time of innocent pleasure and national glory".

Ashley felt forced to make one or two complaints. He was one of those critical people who are essential to every age but not always appreciated. He thought too many firearms were displayed in the exhibition but could not do much about it. He also looked at the words at the head of the catalogue: "The earth is the Lord's and all that therein is." He complained that this version of scripture words was taken from the English Prayer Book and not directly from the Bible.

He was also disgruntled at the way various Bibles had been arranged in a booth. He made sure Bibles would be on show, as the most important and influential of all books. This had not at first been accepted as a very popular idea but he had insisted. He had won agreement but he now found that the Bibles had been arranged in a corner in such a way as to suggest, he thought, that they were secondary to books on art and science.

Ashley made a great fuss; he could be a stickler for details on points he thought were matters of principle. He tried hard to campaign for the observance of Sunday as a special day, attempting to put an end to Sunday mail and on one occasion getting band performances in the parks banned on Sundays. This made him very unpopular and mobs moved up to throw things at his London house. He did not want to stop simple amusements but he believed Sunday was a special day, to be given exclusively to God. He thought people needed a break from work and urged employers to provide a weekly half-holiday.

Sometimes Ashley's principles seemed rather hard for ordinary people to understand. Even Minny sometimes thought he went too far. But if he believed a thing was right, he would not alter his mind. There were few like him.

Something did come out of the exhibition that pleased Ashley very much. Some gentlemen involved in the oversight of the Ragged Schools were looking for good publicity for the schools, through the Great Exhibition. One of them, a man of independent means and also of action, John Macgregor had a good idea. In America he had seen the shoe-black boys who, in those days before casual footwear, could be seen all the time kneeling on the streets polishing American shoes. The equipment was simple and inexpensive and the boys made quite a good living, especially if they looked smart and tidy. Why should English boys not do this for the foreign visitors to the exhibition? Macgregor delighted with his own idea, wrote to Ashley, for his interest in the Ragged Schools was well known.

The idea struck Ashley as very sensible. He at once sent a donation for the new enterprise. When the Great Exhibition opened, a brigade of twenty-five boys, looking smart in simple, neat uniforms, were ready with their brushes and polishers. They were given positions at various strategic spots round the exhibition grounds. On the first day they cleaned more than one hundred thousand pairs of shoes.

This proved such a success that similar brigades were formed in other large cities and the boys, instead of getting mixed up with crime, did an honest job and received reasonable payment. The brigades became quite famous. When Ashley was hurrying to Parliament or anywhere else on important business in the capital city, he would meet the shoe brigade boys and with a smile offer them his feet for a good shoe-shine.

Ashley's life now underwent an important change. His father, with whom he had such an unsatisfactory and shifting relationship, finally died. Ashley, as the eldest son, succeeded to the title and inherited the family properties. He now became the Seventh Earl of Shaftesbury. From then on he was known by the public as Lord Shaftesbury and called Shaftesbury, except within his family where he was still called Ashley. This confused some people, particularly Americans.

He took his new position calmly. It was to bring him quite a few problems. He felt at home with his new title, which he had always known would one day be his. As an Earl he was entitled to wear a coronet on special occasions. This coronet had eight silver balls on stalks alternating with eight gold strawberry leaves. Chief of the properties he inherited was Dorset St Giles, the huge old rosy-bricked mansion he called affectionately "the Saint".

Shaftesbury loved "the Saint". Some of his happiest days had already been spent there. He was proud of the hundreds of years of the history of his family that were wrapped up in the ancient building. It was built principally in the Elizabethan style. He admired the spacious entrance hall the long library and the saloon or Great Hall. He was proud of the family portraits which looked down from the walls and the antiques and works of art which adorned the rooms. He recalled rollicking games and strolls in the pleasure-grounds and happy hours in the shell grotto which was made of ores and minerals from all over the world.

Unfortunately, Shaftesbury's father had rather neglected the main house itself which, being so old, needed constant attention. Instead of regularly renewing crumbling masonry and keeping an eye on poor roofing, he had installed luxuries like new greenhouses and conservatories.

When the details of the Will were sorted out

Shaftesbury realized that along with his new title and properties he had also inherited debts and problems.

The house and the estate servants, many of whom had known him for years, lined up to greet him and the smiling new Countess. The staff looked forward to greatly improved living conditions, especially the estate workers who had realized long ago that nothing would be done for them until the old Earl died. Now they expected something better than their present miserable tied cottages.

Shaftesbury was most anxious to make improvements and to provide superior accommodation and decent wages. But he was as ever hampered by lack of money. He had the authority now but not the cash. He quickly began to do what he could, providing allotments for the workers to grow food and making over land for a cricket ground. But upgrading the tied cottages would prove a long job. "What can I do! The debts are endless!" he cried.

But six months later he had begun to build new cottages and had restored the estate church. He decided that, for the time being and against his personal wishes, he must close St Giles and leave it empty. He could not at that point afford to staff it and live in it.

And what about his London house? The Shaftesbury family mansion in Grosvenor Square in Mayfair, in London's West End, had also become run down and shabby. His parents had chosen not to live there. But it was the family house. So Shaftesbury decided he and Minny and the children would go to live there. He sold the lease of his Brook Street house and with the money renovated the house in Grosvenor Square. He and his family took up residence there. This was the house in which as a child he had been so unhappy and unloved. Now he and Minny would bring warmth and joy to its rooms.

During that momentous year Shaftesbury did not ignore his duties in Parliament. He girded himself for yet another effort on behalf of the chimney-climbing boys – he was always "very worried about my sweeps". He tried to get a law passed which would forbid the employment of any boy under sixteen in the trade. He was successful in the House of Lords but there was still not enough public support in the Commons to get it passed. Shaftesbury almost despaired. He was battling against deep-seated prejudice. But he was determined to keep going.

He had better fortune with a Bill which con-

cerned what were then called Common
Lodging Houses. Many people had to work
away from their homes and these men needed
temporary living accommodation in a lodging
house where they could get food and somewhere to sleep. For ordinary working people
these houses were often awful, dirty and with
insanitary bedding. In Shaftesbury's role as a
Commissioner of the Health Board, he urged
strongly that his Bill be passed. This would
insist on the inspection of the lodging houses
and punishment for those who ran them badly
and exploited the lodgers. He managed to get
this Bill made law and also another Bill that
allowed local councils to put up or buy houses
for the purpose of lodging working people.
Unscrupulous landlords and landladies always
seemed to find ways round Bills, but something was now being done to upgrade the lodging houses and improve public health. At fifty
years old, Shaftesbury was still on the attack.

# 14.

# TO THE HOUSE OF LORDS

The new Seventh Earl of Shaftesbury now had to say goodbye to the House of Commons where he had fought so many battles on behalf of poor and underprivileged people. The chamber of the House had become a second home to him for almost twenty-five years. Now he must leave it behind and take his place in the House of Lords, in its new premises.

The House of Lords, known also as the "Second Chamber" or the "Upper House", was made up of rather special people. Special, that is, because of their rank. They were not elected like members of the House of Commons. There were princes and hereditary peers – that is, the eldest sons of former peers who had taken the family title when their father died. There were the law-lords, the men at the top of the British legal system, and also the "Princes of the Church" – the bishops and archbishops. All the peers of the United Kingdom were entitled to "sit", or attend, in the House of Lords.

The House was not as influential as the House of Commons, where the laws of the land were finally made, but there were many experts in various spheres of knowledge in the "Lords", as well as many men who had nothing much to commend them. These held a position merely as noblemen and owners of great estates. But there was certainly a dignity about the "Lords", with its two impressive carved thrones. The monarch was not permitted to enter the House of Commons but had a right to be present in the Lords.

There was quite a ceremony for the introduction of a new member. The new peer was sandwiched between two sponsors – in earlier times they would have protected him from the sword thrusts of enemies! The three would together march round the "woolsack", where the Lord Chancellor sat, and then return to the bench. Here the new peer in his robes would raise his three-cornered hat three times to the sovereign.

Becoming an hereditary peer and taking his place in the Upper House did not give Shaftesbury much pleasure. In the new premises designed by Barry he looked round at the assembled company and was not impressed.

There were the peers of the realm and the great land and mine owners. Most of them looked half asleep and appeared to have little sense of urgency about the day's business. They seemed rather like members of a comfortable club. Shaftesbury thought the House rather like a "dormitory" and the members like a "gallery of statues", cold and indifferent to the fate of lesser mortals. One peer told him frankly that "there were no sympathies to be stirred in that place". Wistfully, Shaftesbury thought: "The Commons is the depository of power — the peers act as breakwaters!"

This was very depressing but he reminded himself: "God has willed it and I must, and by His Grace will, do my duty." Members of the Commons had said goodbye to him and seen him go, in spite of what they saw as his eccentricities, with a "parting expression of respect and regret".

He could become depressed, even when he had made what he considered a good speech. He wrote in his diary: "Now and then I make a speech which is effective and I get some praise, but the speech is soon forgotten and the man only remembered to be treated as before." This was not entirely true. While the listening members were very wrapped up in their own affairs and rigid views, they grew to respect Shaftes-

153

bury and very often his genuine, enthusiastic and well-prepared approach to issues did win their applause.

When Shaftesbury made his first speech in the Lords there were very few peers present and those who were there were anxious to hurry off to their dinner. But he "found his voice" and got up to speak warmly about his climbing boys. He had a good reception and he "thanked God and took courage".

As he went on making important speeches, the attitude of the peers changed. Although he was a respected man in the prime of life some of them had thought of him as just a "religious eccentric", to be heard mainly promoting his beliefs in church circles or at evangelical public meetings.

It is true that he could be very argumentative and excitable on religious matters and somewhat bigoted in his opinions. Minny often wished he would not get so worked up about things. He had not too great an opinion of professional clergy and longed for the Christian gospel to be offered wherever it could to the poor and unchurched people and for society to be transformed by the conversion of such people. Yet he was displeased by the speeches and activities of the Christian Socialist reformers like Charles Kingsley and F. D. Maurice and refused to work with them. He could not accept the political views through which they expressed their faith. He was also very critical of those who differed from him in their interpretation of the scriptures.

This was an age of fierce argument on religious views and theories. Some of the deepest disagreements were with members of the Tractarian movement. These Christians believed that the national Church was in danger of being swamped by the state. They were deeply concerned for the historic Church and held that the Church was the supreme instrument for good in guiding the nation in the paths of truth. Shaftesbury's cousin, Edward Pusey, was himself a Tractarian.

Of course all these arguments took place because the people who engaged in them cared deeply about their religion, but these matters did greatly affect the life and conduct of the Church at the time. The later idea of ecumenism – church unity – was unthought of. The arguments and discussions were fiery and much time was spent on them. Some of the disagreements were on matters of principle, some seemed to waste a great deal of time on unimportant details.

However, the peers in the House of Lords found that Shaftesbury spoke well, his subjects well researched and his conviction marked. He had developed into an impressive speaker, able to hold his own in any company.

In political terms, Parliament was in a state of flux in those days, with prime ministers coming and going with incredible speed. Within the space of a year or two, Palmerston, Russell, Derby and Aberdeen each took office and left it.

Before leaving the Commons, Shaftesbury had been still worrying about the Factory Act – the famous, or infamous, Ten Hour Bill. It seemed that this was never going to be settled. Although a Bill had been passed, difficulties persisted. Employers searched for ways to get round the Bill and screw more work out of their hapless operatives. One way was to make them work in relays, which the workers hated because this broke up their rest periods. Shaftesbury became really weary, not of the workers and their Bill, but of the endless problems and the attempts of those he saw as greedy manufacturers to evade the provisions of the Bill. He had much to say about it all and became very unpopular at this time. He certainly grew tired and perhaps irritable – people thought that he was for ever going on about the children in the factories.

Also he was not always at ease with Northern people. He did not live near them and, although he visited them when he could, there had never been close relations between the workers' representatives and their great London champion.

They probably felt that Shaftesbury was paternalisitic, treating the adults rather like children. He did not encourage them to take any political action of their own. This was one of the worst times in his life for Shaftesbury – he who cared so much about the workers, particularly the children. He was disgusted with those in Parliament and outside who obstructed his reforms, and he was unhappy with the unhelpful attitudes, as he saw it, of those working for reform among the workers themselves. He was forced to accept that "compromise was still the order of the day" and that the realization of his dreams for the children was still a long way off.

Everyone in public life knows a thrill when power is given to them and during Shaftesbury's life in the House of Lords one such occasion occurred which stirred him deeply. This happened during a time when the Prime Minister was his father-in-law, Lord Palmerston – "Old Pam".

As has been said, these two men would have been expected not to get on, so different were they: Palmerston, the "Regency rake", a man of the world, and Shaftesbury, so deeply and openly religious and disapproving so much of "Pam's" lifestyle. Yet they forged a true friendship. "Pam" was not only fond of Shaftesbury and of course of Minny, who was probably his daughter, but was financially generous to the family. He helped to set young Lionel up in business and gave the job of his private secretary to their third son Evelyn. Now he was more than willing, in fact desirous, of passing on to Shaftesbury one of the duties of Prime Minister that he himself did not welcome.

One of Palmerston's obligations was to appoint high-ranking clergy – bishops, archbishops, deans. Not being in any way religious, Palmerston agreed that he had not the first idea of who to choose. He admitted that he had never spoken to any clergyman except his own parish priest!

Shaftesbury said dryly that Pam did not know the difference between Moses and Sydney Smith – a well-known fashionable cleric of the day. So Palmerston asked Shaftesbury to suggest some names to him.

Of course this delighted the Earl who, being only human, saw this as a chance to give office to men of whom he approved. He saw this of course as being for the good of the Church and the nation. He did not want to see men appointed just because of their family connections or vast learning or fashionable approval. He chose clergy who, as far as he could judge, were faithful shepherds of their flocks, working hard and quietly in their parishes. So he gave various names to Palmerston, who was very grateful as he had to find five archbishops, twenty bishops and thirteen deans.

Palmerston did have some views of his own. He was if anything robustly Protestant and also he did not want any rows with the non-conformist churches but good relations with all. The upshot was the appointment of men often called "the Shaftesbury bishops". They gave satisfaction. At last there were no political appointments or cases of bribery, something not unknown hitherto.

So Shaftesbury settled down in the House of Lords and became an accepted and respected figure there. His home life continued to be very dear to him, though his large family was often a worry. His eldest son was often in debt and the health generally of his sons and daughters also an anxiety. Journeys to warm places in Europe were often a necessity. All this, added to the frightening costs of running the family estates, sometimes plunged him into gloom. But he believed he was trying to carry out God's will and achieved a measure of inward peace. And having at last opened up St Giles, he was happy and content there. Minny was less pleased – perhaps she heard more of the moans of the tenants. A sociable and cosmopolitan creature she really preferred to live abroad.

## 15.

# DEATH OF A HERO

One of Shaftesbury's heroes now died. The Duke of Wellington quietly passed away at Walmer Castle in 1852. He was an old man, over eighty. Shaftesbury had woven in and out of the Duke's life ever since going into Parliament. It was the Duke who had given him, as a very new Member, an influential office on the East India Board of Control. What is more, it was a ministerial job with a salary, Shaftesbury would recall.

Since his boyhood days Shaftesbury had hero-worshipped the Duke. In this respect he stood alongside most Englishmen. To them the Duke was the victor of Waterloo and of the Peninsular War against the French. Wellington had been noted for giving short, sharp but very clear orders. Then he had turned from the laurels of military prowess to the uncertain rewards of parliamentary life – in its way just as dangerous and with many enemies. He was a man of tremendous courage and a great sense of duty.

After his military career, when Wellington became a notable statesman, he managed to keep the common touch. He did not care what people thought if he believed he was right. As he grew older he was to be seen walking to the House, or riding between his home, Apsley House in Hyde Park, to the Horse Guards Parade. People recognized his immaculate, upright figure, his strong profile under his tall hat and his snowy white trousers and tight blue frock-coat. He would always acknowledge the salutes of passers-by.

When Shaftesbury was a young man, newly elected to the House of Commons, the Duke not only gave him a job but showed that he had confidence in this new champion of the poor and wished to help him. He had invited Shaftesbury to visit him on his country estate in Hampshire and as they strolled in the grounds – the upright Duke and his tall young companion – the Duke would reminisce about his campaigns and listen patiently to his young friend's idealistic visions of the future of the nation. There was an affectionate understanding between them.

When Shaftesbury worked for the East India Board, not all his colleagues approved of him, especially of his friendly attitudes to the Indian directors of the board. But whenever they muttered objections, Wellington would support his young protégé.

Later in life Shaftesbury was sometimes puzzled by the Duke's lack of support for certain enterprises dear to his own heart. The Duke was very independent and having made up his mind he changed it rarely – mostly out of a sense of duty.

Several times in his capacity as a statesman the Duke had to support Bills in the House and push them through when he would much rather have not done so.

This was evident in the instance of the Catholic Emancipation Bill. This grand-sounding title covered a parliamentary Bill that was meant to put right an understandable grievance of the Irish people. The Irish, through the Roman Catholic form of Christianity of many of them, were discriminated against in several ways. As the law then stood, they could be represented in the English Parliament only by members of the Protestant minority. This made them furious and the matter was always being brought up.

Now it came to a head. A Liberal Protestant had been selected for their candidate but the fiery Daniel O'Connell had received the most votes from the people. He was a Catholic. His was the voice of the populace but as things stood he could not take his seat in the London Parliament. Things became so bad in Ireland that it looked as if civil war might break out.

Wellington knew he must not allow this to happen. Though himself a convinced Protestant he said: "If I could avoid, by any sacrifice whatever, even one month of civil war . . . I would sacrifice my life in order to do it." So when Sir Robert Peel brought in a Bill to admit the Roman Catholic subjects of the Sovereign to sit in Parliament, to vote at elections and to hold office under the Crown on taking the oath of allegiance to Sovereign and Constitution, the Duke won people over in spite of opposition.

Shaftesbury too, extreme Protestant though he was, also realized that this change had to come. In voting for the new Bill and the new freedom for Catholics he had once again annoyed his father, then still alive, and more unpleasantness had ensued.

The Duke of Wellington was not basically in favour of reform. He felt that on the whole the government of the people was well enough carried out and he did not favour giving "the masses" further representation. He belonged to the old school of aristocrats who believed it was their lot – and their right – to govern, but to do it wisely. A cartoon printed at the time showed the Duke, portrayed as an old dame by the seaside, trying to stem the waves – the rising tide of reform – with a mop!

He was stern with himself and altogether a disciplinarian. Not for nothing was he known as the Iron Duke. The Army which he had served with such distinction was an organization of tough discipline, ruled by the lash. The Emperor Napoleon had been shocked by this – he regarded the methods of discipline of the English armed forces barbarous.

Any move towards greater participation of the people in their own government did not appeal to Wellington. But he observed at all times the concept of "duty" and if told to do something, or if he felt something was right, he obeyed. He had no real wish to take such a large part in politics but when the King asked him to become Prime Minister, he felt he had to say yes.

He was scrupulous in obeying the law. When Shaftesbury had successes with his climbing boys campaign, Wellington ordered builders to change the shape of his own chimneys at Apsley House, to accommodate the new machinery that must now be used in place of the boys. He was no friend of Shaftesbury's Bills but he obeyed the new law.

Wellington was a good landlord on his country estate and was himself a hard worker, carrying on with his parliamentary duties until the end of his long life. At eighty-three he passed quietly away, dying from old age. The poet Tennyson wrote verses about him including the line: "O good grey head which all men knew." This was true. He was a national hero and a familiar one. The rising statesman Benjamin Disraeli said, "He left his country a great legacy – the contemplation of his character."

There was a great national sigh when it was learned that the Duke had gone. He had been a national figure for so long. It was a great personal loss to Shaftesbury who for so many years had benefited from his friendship and patronage. Like Shaftesbury, he had been neglected by his parents; like Shaftesbury he had as a young man "hovered between rather frivolous activities and serious pursuits". His going was a loss.

The lying-in-state of the old Duke took place on the 17th November, 1852. Shaftesbury and Minny went to file past the still figure and they joined the crowds who all wished to show respect. Shaftesbury appreciated these tributes to the old man but was upset by the worldly aspect of the occasion. "What a monstrous misuse of splendour," he confided to his diary. He felt the lying-in-state contained "not a trace of religion". He disliked the display of medals and honours and ribbons.

Shaftesbury was not much more pleased with the Duke's elaborate funeral service. This was an heraldic state funeral, one of pomp and pageantry. Shaftesbury, his wife and his mother-in-law took up positions in St James's Palace from where they had a grand view. They had to be impressed by the procession – "stupendously grand in troops and music" – but Shaftesbury felt it was all too much, especially the gigantic bronze funeral car, 21ft long, which rumbled its slow and majestic way to St Paul's Cathedral. The Earl, who disliked all ritual, felt that all this outward show did little justice to an upright old man – a man who had lived simply though in a grand house and had slept on a small plain iron bedstead. Shaftesbury did not think the Duke would have much appreciated all that was being done in his name.

Shaftesbury was also disgusted at what he saw as the greedy grabbing of various of the Iron Duke's positions and jobs – before he was hardly buried. Many important men were caught up in the frenzied scramble for what Shaftesbury called the "Duke of Wellington's leavings". These included the now vacant position of Commander-in-Chief and Warden of the Cinque Ports. The haste to obtain preferment for these jobs made Shaftesbury shake his head. He felt this was not in keeping with the dutiful, ordered life of the old Duke.

## 16.

# HELPING THE SOLDIERS

Anthony! Anthony! The hearts of Shaftesbury and Minny beat faster. For their sailor son's ship must soon be in danger. And Anthony's life also.

For war broke out in Europe in the middle of the nineteenth century. England and France declared war on Russia. As ever, countries then wheeled and dealed to their own advantage and formed powerful alliances. The Czar of Russia asked Britain to join with Russia in partitioning the country of Turkey but the British did not respond favourably to this. They feared the growth of Russian power and were anxious to maintain Turkey's position on the straits of Bosphorus. This dispute led to war when the Franco-British fleet entered the Black Sea. This conflict was known as the Crimean War.

Turkey was weak at that time and was called the "sick man of Europe". Britain's wish to defend it was popular with the British people who cheered as the troops went off. There was a wave of patriotism.

In those days, for Britain, war was always "far away". Since the threat of invasion had diminished after the Napoleonic wars, battles were always "somewhere else". Communications were not yet fully developed and there were no radio or television links to give quick information. It was to be another twenty years before general use of the telephone.

So news filtered very slowly back to Britain and some people had rather romantic pictures in their minds of the wars – brave soldiers quickly and bloodlessly mopping up the enemy. They had little idea of the horrors of the fighting, the wounds, the fear, the boredom, the general misery. They were wildly patriotic in their wish to send and support the military but knew little of what was actually going on.

Fortunately for the fighting men, there was a voice to speak for them and report events. This voice belonged to William Russell, the war correspondent of *The Times* newspaper. He was able to send back first-hand despatches, though these were slow to arrive, having to travel overland and by sea. At least his reports did enlighten people at home about the progress – and the horror – of the war.

This was a war of long sieges and famous battles. The charge of the Light Brigade at Balaclava, with its terrible British losses, was immortalised in poetry and various names such as Lord Raglan passed into history. But the lot of the ordinary soldiers in the fearful Crimean winter was pitiful. And in helping to lessen their misery it was Shaftesbury, the Seventh Earl, who took a major part.

At first he had been in support of the war. He gradually became disillusioned. He had thought that, as far as was possible, this was a righteous war. Later he was not so sure. He came to the conclusion that the whole operation was badly organized. He was very upset as news filtered through of the disgusting conditions in which the men were bogged down in the Crimean mud in their water-logged trenches. He heard more and more tales of lack of equipment and unbelievable muddle.

What was worse, he heard that when wounded or sick men went into hospital there was very little hope for them there. The main hospital at Scutari was too far from where most of the troops were. It was just a converted barracks built near sewers and cesspools and was vermin-ridden and chaotic. Bare necessities were absent. There was a shortage of all medical equipment, including even simple

items like bandages. Not surprisingly, out-
breaks of disease began, including cholera,
which Shaftesbury had been so quick to attack
in England.

With his keen and tender imagination, he
felt deeply for the poor young men in their
misery and was determined that he would do
something for them. The hard-gained knowledge and contacts acquired when he was a
Commissioner for the Health Board must now
pay off.

Another name now entered the pages of the
time – that of Florence Nightingale. She was
the leisured daughter of a well-to-do family
who had forced her way through nursing training, in spite of heavy opposition. She had
initiated what was to become the modern nursing service. At the beginning of the Crimean
War, Florence had sprung into action and
despite all protests had battled her way with
a small band of dedicated girls to the awful
hospital in Scutari. Here she faced the death-
dealing conditions and set about changing
them. She was a mixture of bossy army general
and angel of mercy and was known by the men
as the Lady with the Lamp as she toured the
hospital wards, not only comforting the

wounded but noting sharply the deficiencies in the building and the nursing facilities.

Florence already knew Shaftesbury and had much respect for him. Together they were able to bring about such changes at the Scutari hospital that the death rate among the soldiers fell dramatically.

Shaftesbury was chatting with a medical friend, a Dr Gavin, a specialist in cholera. The talk turned to the spread of the disease in the Crimea and the poor attempts to control it. Suddenly it was all clear to Shaftesbury – it was he who must do something about it. He at once wrote to Florence Nightingale and their correspondence made clear to him what was really wanted. The next thing was to approach high-ups in England who had the authority to say yes to his requests and actually get things done.

Here Shaftesbury had good fortune. The Government had once again changed and fortunately Lord Palmerston – "Old Pam" – was in office as Prime Minister. Shaftesbury could easily approach his father-in-law and knew he would receive a sympathetic hearing. To his relief, Pam agreed at once with this concern. Both he and his Secretary for War, Lord Panmure, newly in office, were keen to present a caring Government to the people. So they listened thoughtfully. What did Shaftesbury actually have in mind?

Eagerly the Earl poured out his suggestions. His experience with the Health Board enabled him to go straight to the heart of the matter. He suggested that a group of people with powers to inspect and, more important, authority to get things done, should be sent off at once to Scutari. They should talk things over with Miss Nightingale and with the military. "Red tape" must not be allowed to slow things down.

Shaftesbury remembered bitterly all the opposition he had endured years before on the Health Board, when everyone had seemed to be against him – civil engineers, water companies, commissioners of sewers – in fact everyone who had something to gain by leaving things as they were. He was not going to have all this again.

Now all seemed set fair to go ahead. He urged that no time be lost. Astonishingly, within three days, what was called the Sanitary Commission – a group of health workers – had sailed for Scutari. It was made up of two doctors, an engineer and some medical staff from Liverpool. They expected to be gone for two or three months and had full powers to act.

Shaftesbury made it clear that they were to "purify the hospitals, ventilate the ships and exert all that science could do to save life . . ."

At home Shaftesbury waited impatiently for news of some success. At last it came. Despite a number of rows with officials and the need to "pull rank" on the part of the visiting Commission, things had begun to change in Scutari. Workmen had been hired and radical health problems concerned with drains and the hygiene of the hospital buildings were attended to and the water quality checked. Lack of supplies was noted and material ordered, stricter discipline imposed. In fact, quite quickly an altogether different atmosphere prevailed in Scutari.

The wretched war continued and the wounded were still coming in, but the patients' chances of survival were much greater. Between them all – Shaftesbury, Palmerston and Florence Nightingale – the health and care of the fighting men had turned into a major triumph. Afterwards, Florence made it known that she felt a great deal was owed to Shaftesbury in this matter. "That Commission," she wrote to him personally, "saved the British Army."

Shaftesbury had known so many disappointments and apparent failures. He was thrilled and thankful to God that his latest mission had gone well.

The city of Sevastopol was finally taken and Palmerston was able to end the war by the Treaty of Paris in 1856. The Crimean conflict was over. And mercifully Anthony, much-loved son of the Shaftesbury family, was still alive and unharmed.

# 17

# REACHING THE PEOPLE

Every night horse-drawn cabs and carriages drew up outside London's theatres and elegant men and women hurried along to see plays by popular playwrights or musical presentations. At some theatres, middle-class people out for the evening rocked with laughter at the comics or sang and swayed along with performers in the music-halls. Some poorer people climbed the stairs to the gallery where they could look down to the small figures on the stage below and shout out if they were pleased or if they did not approve of what was going on. But for very poor folk the theatre was beyond their means.

Suddenly, it was noticed that on Sunday evenings crowds of shabbily-clad people were making their way to the theatres and actually going inside. This was quite astonishing. Who were they and why were they doing this – on Sunday? Onlookers shook their heads. These people did not look as though they had enough money to buy theatre tickets and were not dressed up for a night out. It was most puzzling.

What was happening was the realization of one of Shaftesbury's dreams – to bring the good news of the Christian faith to the "outsider". Reaching the poor, ordinary, unchurched populace was something seldom out of Shaftesbury's mind and at last he had found a way to start bringing this about.

Why did such people not go to church? Was anything keeping them out? Certainly there was not a great deal to encourage them. Many of the London churches were well-kept, smart buildings and the pews inside had little gates which opened and then clicked shut when the worshippers went in. These worshippers paid pew-rents for their seats, which were then their personal places, where other people did not sit. Apart from having to undo one of the gates and get inside, a visitor to the church might find that he or she could not sit there and this would be embarrassing. And if a church was attended by well-off people dressed in their Sunday clothes, it was not easy for poor shabby folk to feel at home.

All this was apart from the fact that many people knew little or nothing about the Christian gospel, for nobody had taught them or passed on the faith to them. Before the great education bill of later in the century, many of them simply could not read. How could they join in the singing of strange hymns which they could not understand? And they were somewhat put off by the clergymen in their out-of-the-ordinary vestments who, the people thought, would surely be pointing out their misdoings and whose words might mean nothing to them. For the traditional clergyman, such poor people were a "mission-field" and how to set about evangelizing them was a mystery.

Shaftesbury could understand all these factors. He personally was not greatly drawn to clergymen in their traditional role – he thought many of them spent too much time "dressing-up" in their vestments and in the rituals of church services. He thought they should get out and about trying to offer the gospel. So he had the idea of taking the Church to the people if the people did not come to the Church. He was often frustrated by the official activity of the Church of England. "We are all beset and bound in the church by starch and buckram just as all the departments of the government are under the bondage of red tape," he declared irritably.

Shaftesbury and some supporters hit on the

idea of meeting in the Exeter Hall, a large building in London's Strand. This could take several thousand people and seemed ideal. The hall was much favoured for meetings where evangelical speakers promoted various church and charitable causes, especially in the month of May. Once, in spite of it being frowned upon, the Queen's husband, Prince Albert, was persuaded to take the chair there as President of the Labourers' Friend Society.

Shaftesbury himself once spoke at the hall. He got on his "hobby horse" and launched into an attack on what he called Ritualists – people of High Church persuasion. These were used to services with robed priests, with incense and with much bowing of the knee and making of the sign of the cross. Shaftesbury was rather unreasonable on these matters, though he could not see this in himself. So he roared out: "I would rather worship with Lydia on the bank by the riverside than with a hundred surpliced priests in the temple of St Barnabas."

This was a reference to the story in the Acts of the Apostles about the Early Church meeting in the open air and being the guest of the cloth-seller Lydia. Shaftesbury thought this preferable to taking part in an elaborate church service.

He was even upset because at a service in

the church of St Alban, Holborn, people going up to Holy Communion moved forward to the sound of soft music. Shaftesbury felt this was theatrical.

He wished every aspect of Christianity to be plain and simple. Apparently a lot of people agreed with him for when he sat down after his speech there was "a thunder of applause".

The twentieth-century idea of ecumenism, of trying to unite the different branches of the Christian Church, would have astonished him. The idea was then far, far off. He did not wish to be unpleasant and dictatorial, but he thought he was fighting for the right. He was a creature of his age when religious people spent much time in argument. But he never went to lengths of persecution as sometimes happened when devout Christians became religious fanatics. He was basically too kindly a person for that.

Booking the Exeter Hall for services was not straightforward. Blocking it was a very old Act of Parliament. This said it was against the law for more than twenty people to meet for public worship in a building not specially licensed for it. This old law was not often used, but it had been revived to prevent meetings arranged by the workers of the London City Mission.

Shaftesbury thought this an absurd law and said it had to go. He could not understand anyone objecting to people meeting together anywhere when their only aim was to worship God. But he understood that some clergymen felt their authority threatened.

Finally some alterations were made to the old law and it became possible for services to be held in the Exeter Hall. With great excitement Shaftesbury and his friends took the next step of advertising the services by means of large posters and by sending out invitations to all and sundry. It was understood that anyone, however poor, was welcome at these services and that no one would ever be embarrassed.

Would anyone come? It was an anxious time of prayer and hope for Shaftesbury and his supporters. Would their faith be justified?

It was a great joy and relief to him when crowds of people thronged the pavement outside the Exeter Hall and after a few moments of hesitation disappeared inside. They did not know quite what to expect but, after all, they had little money for outings on a Sunday evening and this might make a change from sitting at home. Some went out of curiosity, perhaps some just to jeer.

Whatever their feelings, when they got inside they sensed an air of excitement. Most

soon found themselves involved in the simple
services and decided to come again. They sat
comfortably on seats instead of in stiff pews.
There were no reserved seats – and no collec-
tions. No one urged them to keep quiet before
events began and when the service did start
they found it understandable. There was some
hearty singing, though mostly by middle-class
churchgoers who had come to support. Plain,
simple prayers were said – in words that they
could understand and that had meaning for
their lives.

Short Bible passages were read effectively,
then someone came to the platform and talked
to them about the offer of Christ. These were
specially-chosen speakers. The visitors
learned, many for the first time, that Christ
loved each one of them and that each one of
them was utterly precious to Him. This was a
revelation. Most of them thought that nobody
much cared about them. They had value!
Somebody did care about them! Each one could
know the Saviour personally.

They would leave the Exeter Hall feeling
quite uplifted. And they had enjoyed their
night out. It had been "different" but it had
been a night of good companionship. In spite
of the misgivings of the hall-manager, there
had been no rough behaviour. Nobody had

needed to be thrown out. There had been a general atmosphere of reverence. Sometimes this "congregation" even broke into clapping and cheering. Shaftesbury was overcome with emotion and told his diary that the enthusiasm of the people was "miraculous". Sometimes so many came to the services that, reluctantly, some had to be turned away . . .

Unfortunately, the vicar of the parish in which the Exeter Hall stood grew offended by the great numbers attending the gatherings. He changed his mind about agreeing to these services. As the law was still something of a muddle, the Bishop of London was forced to forbid the Hall services to go on. Some of the nearby churches, seeing how the poor people had flocked to the simple services, opened their own doors more widely and made it easier for new worshippers to come in.

Shaftesbury, very annoyed at the decision to refuse the Exeter Hall meetings, made his boldest move yet. He hired seven theatres in London for the services. Some of these buildings were in the poorest and most unsavoury parts of London. He believed that the poorest and roughest of the people would not be afraid to go inside and he was right. The famous theatre, the Old Vic, where rumbustious low-class entertainment was the usual fare at that time and which was notorious for the presence of riff-raff, was a theatre Shaftesbury did not scorn. In this unlikely place people crowded the stalls, the pit and the galleries and were never nervous or uncomfortable. Here among rough neighbours and the smell of well-worn clothing and sometimes of unwashed bodies or of drink, Christ was offered and found. The Saviour who came for the outsider and the rejected became real to many who had never bent their head or the knee in worship before.

Shaftesbury and his friends and colleagues were thrilled at the big congregations in the theatres and believed that these attendances must make a difference to the life of the nation. He stood up in the House of Lords to tell his hearers all about these services, a brave thing to do, and he emphasized how reverent the congregations were, remembering that they had beforehand had no idea of how to behave in church. And, more important, he spoke of the effect upon the people of the simple but deep message of the good news of the gospel that was being so dramatically given to the poor.

"Look at the great things that have been done," he urged, rejoicing. His fight for the poor had taken an unusual and effective turn.

As he said, "The Early Christians converted heathen shrines to Christian use – why not use theatres?"

## 18.

# A WORLDWIDE OUTLOOK

The last years of Lord Palmerston's time as Prime Minister saw Britain at peace with herself – prosperous, and the hub of a burgeoning Empire. The arts and crafts flourished. The Pre-Raphaelite painters were important, the poets Tennyson and Browning found fame. Anthony Trollope and Charles Dickens achieved popularity with their novels. And, of the utmost interest to Shaftesbury, the scientist Darwin propounded his theories of evolution. There was much intellectual ferment and vigour.

Abroad, however, the ferment was on a more violent scale. There was scarcely a country where there was not some kind of agitation going on. Often blood was spilt. Shaftesbury was intensely concerned with all this. He longed for a totally Christian world and his sympathy with human beings of all races stretched far beyond his native shores. He held strong opinions and frequently allied himself to the causes of other nations. This sometimes caused Minny and his in-laws to sigh: "Please don't take on any more interests!"

He travelled most years to Europe, often for family health reasons, and knew Europe well. He was always ready to help Protestant minorities if he felt they were being persecuted. His name and his position were guarantees of his sincerity and his influence.

The Italians were struggling for independence. In those days Italy was divided up into different states and tyranny often reigned. Britain had strong public sympathies with this struggle but was not officially involved. However, cordial expressions of sympathy in Foreign Office despatches encouraged the liberators. Shaftesbury felt that, in the sympathy he showed, he was speaking for most English people. He was a close friend of the Sardinian Minister in London and knew much of what went on behind the scenes.

He was delighted when, in 1860, the Italian liberator Garibaldi took his great step to free the government and drew Italy together. Within the next ten years the Italian-speaking peoples were united.

Farther afield he also identified with the struggle of the Polish people for a national identity. An almost schoolboyish sense of adventure drew him to support movements he believed were morally right. Likewise he threw himself into a campaign against reported Bulgarian atrocities in the Balkans. He wrote strong letters to *The Times*.

Some of his fiercest feelings and most ardent support were directed towards the New World. The beginning of the American Civil War caused him to think through his priorities. He would buttonhole people with his views on the subject almost to the point of boredom.

This infamous war was waged basically on the threat of the secession of the southern states from the United States of America. Indirectly of course the cause was slavery – the southern states still owning and using slaves.

Shaftesbury felt hotly about the topic. He knew that in the hundred years between 1680 and 1780 the British slave trade had shamefully shipped two million slaves from Africa to the West Indies. This terrible practice had been outlawed in the British Empire in 1807, when Shaftesbury was a little boy, and by the time he entered Parliament slavery had finished. But he knew that, in the American deep south, it was still a major issue.

This horrified him. He knew, as a Christian, that all men are born free. He had read the popular book *Uncle Tom's Cabin*. This book by the American author Harriet Beecher Stowe about a runaway slave was being much discussed and argued about. It moved Shaftesbury deeply.

He set about organizing a British campaign to support the Abolitionists, as the party was called, which demanded freedom for the slaves. He often held lonely opinions and he believed that the northern and southern states of the Union with their differing views would live more amicably if they were separate. He thought it a disaster to try to draw together states with such opposing ideas. Few people supported him in this and he annoyed many Americans who did not share his views.

The plight of countries even farther away intrigued Shaftesbury and sometimes caused him to get excited. He was very upset at the outbreak of the two "opium wars" waged against China. He thought them mean wars, forced on China.

These wars were fought to enforce the opening up of Chinese ports to British trade, especially the trade in opium, a horrible addictive drug. The opium was grown in British India and its enforced sale was to pay for the items Britain brought in from China – silk, porcelain and especially tea. Officials declared that unless Britain could exchange trade with China, she would not be able to pay for her imports. China had long considered herself the "Middle Kingdom" and was self-sufficient and wished to have nothing to do with the Western world, which she considered a race of barbarians. She was most reluctant to open her ports. The result was a nasty war.

In the second opium skirmish, Britain allied herself with France and the whole business ended with the setting on fire of the Summer Palace in Peking.

Shaftesbury thought – and said – that the opium trade was totally disgraceful. He believed the two wars were a shame on Britain's good name. Until the end of his life he was President of the Anti-Opium League.

He also had something to say publicly in 1877 when Queen Victoria was declared Empress of India. He was not pleased. He thought this title had a "military, despotic, offensive air". Early in his parliamentary life he had become interested in India, when he had held a ministerial post on the India Board. Admiration and affection had grown for the Indian people and he had urged promotion for Indian officials. It was always his hope that Christianity would spread throughout India and that the people might, of their own free will, turn away from their national gods to the one true God. So he never lost his concern for this great nation.

He had also always been interested in the plight of the Jewish people. He now found out about a pogrom – a systematic massacre and plunder of Jewish people – by the Russian Tzarist government. Alarmed and dismayed, he quickly became President of a Relief Committee to raise funds for helping those Jews who wished to emigrate to Europe. Hard work for this cause was carried out in a special office opened near the Houses of Parliament.

Obstinacy was one of his characteristics and he could be single-minded and determined in his opinions. Sometimes he could be stubbornly against his Government. In later years he was much opposed to the "spirited foreign policy" of Prime Minister Disraeli.

Known as "Dizzy", Disraeli was in favour of extending Britain's power and securing British interests in India. The town of Quetta was taken and an Embassy ordered to be set up in Kabul, the capital of Afghanistan. This was mountainous, landlocked country in south central Asia. A mission of a thousand mostly armed men – really a small army – set off for Kabul but was repulsed on the Khyber Pass.

An ultimatum was sent. No reply was

received. Then British soldiers were ordered to invade Afghanistan. This caused fierce argument in Britain, with some people pleased, others, like Shaftesbury, very upset. He was urged to join a group against the new war. He would not do this. He did not like the idea of washing one's dirty political linen in public, or getting the Foreign Office involved in a public wrangle. But he said plenty in an outspoken way and condemned Disraeli for what he saw as a needless war.

At the same time, Shaftesbury paid close attention to what was going on his own much-loved land. He could not approve of everything the masses did and thought. He found the desire of the people for an extension of voting rights unpalatable. If ordinary working people gained too much say over the decisions of government, who knew what might not happen?

As he grew older his opinions grew more set and he was sometimes left behind in his thinking by younger activists with more radical views. He found, as everyone does, that his own grown-up sons tended to smile at his views. But as he aged he did not find it easy to change. So he had to accept that in 1867 a new Reform Bill was made law. This gave the vote to all male householders in towns and also lodgers who paid £10 a year in rent. In the counties men occupying a house worth £12 a year also got the vote. The population was on the way to universal franchise – voting for everybody. But it was to be many years before women were included as voters.

# 19.

# FAMILY MATTERS

Whatever the crises of public life, Shaftesbury did not allow them to overwhelm his devotion to his large family and to his estates. Most of his living children were now grown-up. The eldest, Accy, was always a worry, liable to get into debt and easily influenced, though pleasant and kindly. It was accepted that he would probably continue to need support. Accy obtained a parliamentary seat though he did not distinguish himself. Within a few years he and his wife would have a son who would be the first heir to the Earldom to be born at St Giles.

Other sons were rewarding in their lifestyle. Evelyn, secretary to Lord Palmerston, was later called to the Bar. Lionel was active in a business career. Young Cecil, still at home, was a rather delicate schoolboy. He was often invited to play games with the royal children in the gardens of Buckingham Palace. Both Evelyn and Lionel had married and their wives pleased Shaftesbury and Minny.

The girls of the family grew up to be charming and delighted their parents with their unselfish natures. All four daughters visited the local hospital to read to disabled people. But neither Vea nor Conty was outwardly as attractive as their mother and they were not pursued by suitors. Perhaps their obvious lack of dowries might have put off some young men in an age when marriage settlements were still part of the joining of great families.

The parents were worried about the future of these girls who, of course, followed no careers. There was no training for such young ladies and if they did not marry they would be expected to remain at home.

Shaftesbury, so easily despondent, brooded about this. In time Vea did marry happily.

The girls were not very robust. So many young ladies of the day were "delicate" – laced up in their Victorian corsets they easily fell prey to diseases not yet fully understood. They seldom took enough exercise. Son Maurice had died in Switzerland in 1855 and Mary, a victim of lung disease, would follow him within a few years.

The health of the family was a great concern for Shaftesbury. Warmer climates seemed essential to all of them and each year several of them joined Shaftesbury and Minny in a trip to the health spa at Ems in Germany. Here they "drank the waters" which was thought helpful in those days. Minny loved to travel and always brightened up when abroad. Her husband found this an irksome interruption to his busy life but was convinced the trips were necessary. Unfortunately, his absences on these health journeys were not always understood and brought criticism that he was less often seen on the estate than was to be expected.

He loved his old home and relished every moment there. But he was deeply worried at the debts he incurred every time he tried to put something right on the estate. In the past he had been much helped by generous money gifts from his sister Caroline and his mother-in-law, Lady Palmerston. But as these ladies passed on and after financial problems with an unprincipled agent, he was forced to accept an interest-free loan from staunch friends. This went against the grain but there was no alternative. He sold some of the family jewellery, pictures and silver plate. But he did not want to denude the fine old mansion of all its treasures.

It was delightful to see the estate tenants so pleased when improvements were made to their cottages. And St Giles itself, the ancestral home, was gradually restored and improved. Land drainage schemes were put in hand and a covered walk laid down. A "bust" was set up, a head and shoulders statue of Lord Shaftesbury himself. This had been given to Minny by grateful workers in the factories of the North and had been presented to her in Manchester. She was very proud of it. The Elizabethan stables were restored and all in all the master was once again proud of his "dear old saint". The young people were happy here and also when visiting their grandparents at Broadlands in Romsey, where they were always welcome.

Shaftesbury also felt some responsibility for the way the tenants lived. He thought some of the young men were coarse and brutal in their speech and behaviour and spoke to the rector of the parish about it. He was also indignant if, having been given better accommodation, the tenants did not look after it. He cared so much about them.

Shaftesbury could be comparatively serene in the surroundings of his old home, but he was still liable to fits of depression and also to becoming unwisely intense in some aspects of his life. This caused irritation among his relatives and friends. In 1855 Palmerston offered him the Duchy of Lancaster and Shaftesbury promptly refused. This annoyed Pam and led to a serious family row. There were sometimes disagreements with Minny when she felt he was too much wrapped up in his activities and becoming too worried. This led to an unusual coolness between them.

One of the more heightened disagreements occurred when the Queen offered Shaftesbury the Order of the Garter. This was and is the senior British Order of Knighthood, founded by Edward III in 1347 and a gift made personally by the Sovereign. Shaftesbury had already once refused the gift, thinking it had political links, and this had upset Minny, who was friendly with the Queen. He now wished to brush it aside once more, partly because accepting the honour brought certain expense. But Minny and Palmerston between them persuaded him that this would really offend the Queen. So he finally agreed to accept it.

The Order has a distinctive badge, a garter of dark blue velvet with the motto of the Order in gold lettering *Honi soit qui mal y pense* – 'Shame to him who thinks evil'. It is worn by gentlemen below the left knee on formal knee breeches. It was and is something very special. Minny and Lady Palmerston and Old Pam were all relieved that Shaftesbury had not proved too obstinate and they knew that Queen Victoria herself, now a sad widow, was pleased at his acceptance. What was more, Palmerston quietly paid the necessary expenses for his son-in-law; he never stinted in generosity to the Shaftesbury family.

Shaftesbury was now becoming an old man. He had less energy and was extremely deaf. But he still found life worthwhile and was committed to many good causes. He did not think God had dismissed him from his fight for justice and a good quality of life for the poor. So he soldiered on, pushing the years aside. He still strode through the slums to see the situation for himself.

In his personal life, like most people, he knew both joys and sorrows. He suffered the loss by death of many of those closest to him. In a space of twenty years he was bereft of Old Pam, his mother-in-law Lady Palmerston, his daughter Conty and, worst of all, his beloved wife Minny. These were hard blows and it took all Shaftesbury's Christian faith to bear them.

He had always regretted the easy-going lifestyle of his in-laws but could not deny their great kindness to him and his family. When Old Pam died, Shaftesbury lost not only an affectionate friend but also a patron. Palmerston had lent an ear to important issues that his son-in-law wanted to discuss and his influence had been vital to Shaftesbury. Now he was gone. And Lady Palmerston's sweet, generous disposition had always been a support. She had always been "Dear, kind, Mum" and would be sadly missed.

The loss of his daughter Conty, whom he had nursed tenderly, was another blow. But the bitterest was to have Minny taken from him. He could hardly put into words what he thought about her and what he believed she had been to him. Minny had overtaxed her strength in caring for her sick daughter Mary and had died quietly at their house in London.

Shaftesbury would remember words he had written in his diary at the time of his marriage. Having asked God for "a wife for my comfort, improvement and safety" he had gone on to write: "He has granted me to the full all that I desire and far more than I deserved. Praised be His Holy Name." After all these years of married life he could still say Amen to that. "God permitted me to live with her for two and forty years," he wrote.

Minny, in a marriage where neither family had approved of the other, had lived with a good, often saintly man, but a man with a difficult temperament. He could be moody and depressed, often excitably obsessed, with exactingly high standards, and always short of money. She had borne and brought up a family of ten children, with much family illness. Above all, she had practised a gentle Christian faith and brought a bright and sunny nature to her married life. She had acted as an elegant society hostess and wise family counsellor and was loved by all. She had been everything to her husband and now he had to go on without her. He had no doubts, though, that she would be received in heaven as a truly Christian wife and mother.

He received a sympathetic letter from the widowed Queen, who could understand so well what he was going through. She had been very fond of Minny.

Shaftesbury did not allow his private griefs to dominate his public life. He continued with his duties and gradually resumed a single social life. He enjoyed the visits of his young grandchildren to St Giles and once again the old mansion echoed with the happy laughter of "the kids" and the whoops of joy as they scuttled down the long corridors playing hide and seek or rushed about in the grounds. They saw that their grandfather was immensely tall and stately, with his iron-grey hair and lined face, but they were not frightened of him. His blue eyes would often twinkle and his affection for them was obvious. They knew that Grandfather loved all children and constantly proved it by the way he lived.

They heard that he had gone to visit one of the Ragged Schools he cared so much about, where he found many of the children genuinely hungry. At once he had said that pious words were not enough. He had given orders for huge quantities of soup to be boiled up in his own London kitchens and distributed to the hungry children and their mothers and fathers.

Shaftesbury was always wanting to give away money and goods and to help people in a practical way. He was as usual frustrated by lack of funds. To his amazement and delight a complete stranger left a huge sum of money for him to distribute to needy causes. At first the whole task seemed too great and he suggested to his lawyer that the matter be left to executors, as was allowed for in the Will. But he was persuaded that a more personal touch was needed. He sat down and thought and made a long list of people and institutions who would benefit from this wonderful gift. It was a tiring business but very encouraging and satisfying.

At St Giles, where he went in the parliamentary recess, he lived very simply, not bothering much with the great state rooms but living mostly in his den, where his books were. He slept in a plain iron bed, much like the one favoured by his hero the Duke of Wellington. In his den many prayers were said and decisions reached. With his dogs around him, supportive servants and the love of the tenants on the estate, and frequently visited by his family, he kept going.

It can be said that Shaftesbury had a huge extended family, particularly the young people he cared about. In the Boys' Refuge in a slummy part of London, an amazing scene took place one day. More than a hundred boys were tucking into what was probably the best meal they had ever eaten. Their table manners were not stylish, but they showed their approval as they tackled with relish the ample meat and vegetables set before them, followed by lashings of pudding. There were murmurs of pleasure as they devoured their meal.

At the back of the shabby hall stood Shaftesbury, smiling broadly, and the helpers who had prepared and served the meal. Almost two hundred lads had accepted the invitation to this meal and now they were being shepherded into an adjoining room where Shaftesbury waited to talk to them. They quietened down, the jokes and laughter dying away. What did the Earl want with them? They were silent before this tall formidable presence whom they had seen from time to time in their Ragged Schools. His was a kindly face but he had authority and they listened carefully. None of the boys was over sixteen and they were all poor and shabbily-dressed.

Shaftesbury asked them a searching question. How many of them had ever been in prison? He wanted a truthful answer. After a moment's hesitation a number of hands went up. Some admitted to more than one term in gaol. They were then asked how they got a daily living if they were honest. They answered: they held horses, begged, or cleaned boots. It was all rather pathetic. When the Earl asked them if they would really like a life that was different and did not get them into trouble with the law, most nodded vigorously.

To their surprise, Shaftesbury then put before them a vision of a large ship, anchored in the River Thames, where as many as a thousand boys could be put on board and taught a trade. Such boys could be trained for the Royal Navy or the Merchant Service. How did the idea of such a life appeal to them? Who would be interested?

At once dozens of hands shot up and looks of excitement appeared on the young faces. Did the Earl really mean all this? He nodded and told them to wait and see. The boys ran off chattering excitedly to one another. Many had only the most rudimentary shelter, perhaps under a tarpaulin or a pile of boxes. Many had no proper homes.

Once again, Shaftesbury took action. The Royal Navy and the Merchant Navy, after wartime service, now had too many ships and not enough people to sail in them. It was a good time for this scheme of Shaftesbury's to work. He held discussions with officials and before long the Lords of the Admiralty had allotted to his scheme a fifty-gun sail-rigged frigate, the *Chichester*. The public, hearing of this venture and being drawn into Shaftesbury's enthusiasm, gave sufficient contributions to fit out the ship.

Arrangements were then made to contact the boys and without much delay two hundred lads arrived to begin a new life on the *Chichester*. The Earl believed that this life would be healthier and happier for the boys than their days of petty crime in the city slums. On the ship the boys would be educated in seamanship and also in the Christian faith so that they could turn out to be an asset to their country, a country in which so far they had neither received nor given much.

The sailing boys scheme was a great success and a few years later a second ship, the *Arethusa*, was brought into service.

Shaftesbury also thought of those boys and girls who were not able to go to sea. For those among them – a fearfully large number – who were homeless, he set up national refuges, later known as Shaftesbury Homes, where they could be cared for and later placed in some kind of work, either at home or abroad. He could not see need before his eyes without doing something about it.

## 20.

# STILL FIGHTING

Towards the end of his long life Shaftesbury could be found still carrying the discipline of a busy working existence and still fighting for the poor and underprivileged.

Some of the issues for which he had struggled and fought for so long still surfaced from time to time. They had not all been permanently resolved. So he breathed a sigh of relief when in 1875 a Bill was passed which for ever ended the scandal of the sweep climbing boys. It was now many years since he had cried, "I'm worried, worried about my climbing boys." The new Act forbade any sweep to carry on his trade without a licence from the police and the police could enforce the provisions of the Act. So at long last, after a terrible battle, small boys from poor homes were now safe from the fear of the deadly chimneys. Shaftesbury was seventy-four years old. He had persisted for decades to see this fight come to victory.

The fight to help the factory workers had

also proved a continuing hassle. Now a further Act tidied up many of the existing injustices and benefited many workers who had previously been left out of the regulations.

Several important politicians who had opposed Shaftesbury's Bills through the years now admitted that they had been wrong and agreed that Shaftesbury had done a marvellous job. It was said that he did more than any other one man to check the power of the mighty industrial machine in Britain. It had all proved exhausting for him and had swept him from the path of traditional career politics. But he believed it had been worthwhile. It had been, he thought, what a Christian gentleman must do.

New ventures still called him. People had only to ask for help and he would not refuse. And as usual he would not simply give his name to an appeal or organization but had to look thoroughly into it and get involved in a practical way. Some of these new interests brought him much cheer.

One such was unique to London and revolved round the city's street traders, known as costermongers. These men and women of London's mean streets were a close-knit clan who supported one another like a large family. They made their living selling mainly fruit and vegetables from barrows drawn by donkeys. The costers, as they were often called, were not among the very poorest in the city but they were not well off, often sharing their dwellings and their donkeys, and bore many hardships.

For one thing they had to save up enough money to purchase their donkey and barrow and of course to continue to feed the animal. Not surprisingly many of the donkeys, like their owners, were rather thin and bony. Costers also claimed that they were often harassed by the police. They were independent-minded men and women, unbowed by their circumstances, and mostly very cheerful. They were well known for their colourful language but were basically good-hearted. On special occasions they wore waistcoats and large hats trimmed with pearl buttons. They elected leaders known as the Pearly King and Pearly Queen.

Shaftesbury met them through a young man called Will Orsman who had been converted to the Christian faith and had begun a small mission in Golden Lane. Here he offered the gospel in an ordinary room and found he could attract the costers to his simple meetings and that they felt at home with him. He also tried to help them in practical ways. Shaftesbury found all this most intriguing and was soon enrolled as an honorary coster. He joined the Donkey and Barrow Club which Orsman started to help costers to save for an animal and a cart.

Shaftesbury took delight in buying his own donkey and cart and having his family coat of arms stamped on the cart. He would lend them out to costers who could not yet find the full amount to purchase for themselves. These men and women would smile as they drove off with the noble coat of arms on the side of their barrow.

Shaftesbury loved animals – horses and dogs held high place on his estates – and detested what he saw as cruel field sports. He acted as Vice President of the Royal Society for the Prevention of Cruelty to Animals. He did his best to explain to his coster pals that donkeys should be well treated and that this was the secret of getting the best from them.

To his surprise, at a jolly gathering of costers with their donkeys he was presented with the gift of a splendid animal for himself. It was a fine specimen and he was delighted. This donkey was sent to live in comfort at St Giles where it was a loved friend to the Shaftesbury grandchildren who gave it titbits and rubbed its soft furry ears. Shaftesbury was pleased at this mark of affection from a fine body of working people.

Another new campaign brought less jollity. Once again he had to summon up energy and stand up against snubs and sneers. Once more he was up against bad customs, and systems that touched people's purses. He was never popular when this happened. Once again he was fighting for the poor and the children of the poor.

This time it concerned the land, though not the part of England that he himself knew well. He had discovered shocking practices in the eastern counties, the flat agricultural areas where, in those days, so much of the work was labour-intensive, requiring numbers of casual workers to do seasonal jobs.

The system which Shaftesbury now had to fight was that of gang labour on the farms. A farmer would pay a gang-master to get for him the labour that he needed for a particular job, such as setting potatoes or weeding. So the boys and girls of the poor were sent by their parents to form part of the gangs, about forty children in each mixed gang.

All was not well with this system. Most of the children were young – one was known to have been only six years old. Not surprisingly she collapsed quite soon. The children worked long hours and many had to walk a distance to work. Some were known to have covered sixteen miles a day there and back to work. Some of the gang-masters were very rough with the children and some were known to have abused their charges. The children were at the mercy of the gang-masters and many suffered. In the area round the rural town of Wisbech there were nearly as many infant deaths as in the huge industrial city of Manchester. It was time for something to be done.

Getting rid of these horrid practices was a real effort for the Earl. The Government, as so often, was slow to want to change anything and Shaftesbury's first attempt to bring in a new Bill was a failure. So was a second Bill brought in by another Member. At last, a new Act of Parliament said No to the use in the gangs of children under ten. But there were still grumbles from some members of the House of Lords, who did not like their estate working to be interfered with and did not like Shaftesbury meddling in their affairs.

It has to be remembered that these were rough days in general, but was there no end to the nasty conditions in which children were made to work? It had not happened yet, thought the Earl. For yet another horrible life-style for children had been brought to his notice.

This time it centred on the country's brick-fields. A man called George Smith sent Shaftes-bury a leaflet in which he was trying to stir up indignation at the plight of the brickfield children. Smith himself had been one of their victims as a child. This sent the Earl scurrying down to one of the brickworks. Here he, who was so used to awful sights, saw yet one more.

The brickfield was a nasty mess of great lumps of wet, dripping clay. Little children, almost naked, were staggering towards the firing kilns with huge armfuls of the heavy, sticky stuff clasped to their bodies. Shaftesbury declared they "looked like pillars of clay". When the children tottered to the kilns where they had to put the wet clay down, the heat was terrible. "I was not able to remain for more than two or three minutes," Shaftesbury later told the House of Lords.

He brought the matter dramatically before them. He said plainly the brickfields were "a disgrace to the country". He was heard in silence. Of course before any Bill could be passed it had to be introduced in the Commons and the Liberal Member for Sheffield wrestled to achieve this victory. At last it became against the law to employ children in the brickfields. Another success – but again at an exhausting price.

Shaftesbury was becoming a really old gentleman now. His tall form was bent and furrows appeared on his fine-featured face. From various disabilities he suffered a good deal of pain. But he could still smile at his grandchildren and indeed any child that passed by.

When he could spare the time he went to St Giles, where he was at peace. Early each morning he would stroll through the grounds to the lake and see the wild fowl fly down and the ducks crowd up to be fed. He would hold family prayers each morning, reading from the Bible and offering simple prayers. Afterwards the dogs would bound in and keep him company. He still endured "roaring in the ears" and his deafness made public life difficult.

His family was attentive and he was well looked after by his unmarried daughter Hilda. But he greatly missed Minny and all his friends who had gone. Occasionally he would accept an invitation to dinner. He was invited to dine with the Princess Mary Adelaide, the granddaughter of King George III. The Earl rather dreaded this kind of evening as the Princess, a lady of stout proportions, liked to linger on at the dining table. Poor Shaftesbury was always nearly asleep when she rose and signalled to go to the drawing room. On one such visit he could stand it no longer. When the meal ended he got up abruptly and left the table with a bow, horrifying the courtiers.

Brief holidays apart, such as visiting Scotland which he loved, the Earl continued his orderly life of helping people. "I must work as long as life lasts," he insisted.

Sometimes assistance was given on his very doorstep, when poor people called in distress and were offered food and other help. Relentless demands were still made on him.

He became what a century later might be called an "Ombudsman" – examining problems and coming up with solutions. So people brought to him the plight of merchant seamen in their "coffin ships", so low in the water with their cargoes as to be dangerous. Action here resulted in the bringing in of the Plimsoll line on ships, which marks the safe level of the ships in the water.

Some invited the Earl to join the movement to prevent animals being used for experiments. Someone else brought to his notice the difficulties of some acrobat children. Some asked him to agitate on behalf of girl children traded abroad as prostitutes. He never said no – he took up all these causes. He fought on.

On a spring morning, 28th April, 1881, Shaftesbury awoke feeling an unusual sense of excitement. What was the day to bring? Then it came flooding into his mind – it was his eightieth birthday and it was going to be a very special day.

There was a desire for a national celebration but the initiative was taken up by the Ragged Schools Union, who had so much to thank the Earl for. Knowing that crowds of people would want to come to the great gathering planned for the occasion, the Lord Mayor of London offered the use of the London Guildhall for the event. The Lord Mayor was a convinced Christian and he and his lady were determined to be present themselves.

The Guildhall, probably second only to the Tower of London as a great historic building, was open in all its splendour for the birthday hero. As Shaftesbury, walking rather slowly, entered the building, members of the Flower Girls' Mission ran up and scattered flowers before him on the path. Inside, many people wanted to get up and speak to pay tribute to the man they admired and loved so much. There was a very mixed crowd, with poor people from all the groups associated with the

Earl and also some important public figures. Shaftesbury could not help noticing that several VIPs who had received invitations had declined them. Perhaps, he thought wryly, these mighty ones did not want to be linked with the Ragged Schools Union!

Shaftesbury was delighted with this reception and was given the gift of a large portrait of himself. Privately he also received masses of appreciative mail. Among all the formal letters and addresses from public bodies was a simple note from his sister Charlotte, now an old lady. It touched his heart. It read: "May God continue to watch over your most precious life." Their relationship had always been affectionate.

The celebrations continued. Another big gathering was held in Manchester. Shaftesbury had already received the Freedom of the City of Glasgow. Now at the end of his life he was given the Freedom of the City of London, the capital of which he had been such a distinguished citizen. The Freeman's casket presented to him was of gold in a finely wrought design.

So Shaftesbury had many signs to remind him of the admiration and love in which he was held. He would never forget this.

But the years were catching up with him. In

July 1885 he spoke at the first annual meeting of the National Society for the Prevention of Cruelty to Children. Could there have been any cause closer to his heart! This was to be his last public speech. He was eighty-four years old. He said afterwards, "I find myself simply an old man who has endeavoured to do his duty in that state of life to which it has pleased God to call him . . ."

Shaftesbury left for a little holiday and some sea-air in Folkestone. Here he fell ill, too unwell to be taken back to his beloved St Giles. He would certainly have wished to be there at the end of his life. But he knew, as all Christians do, that it does not matter where we are when we die – we are in God's hands. So when his family came to visit him, they found him calm and peaceful.

He told a friend, "I know that my Redeemer liveth and that He has been my Friend for many years." In this confident spirit, Shaftesbury took his last breath.

It was his belief that he would meet in Heaven the "little band" of his family who had already gone on before – Francis, Maurice, Mary, Conty, Minny. He was confident that they were all safe in the arms of the Lord.

# EPILOGUE

Shaftesbury was laid to rest at Dorset St Giles – his "dear old saint" – alongside his wife and the children who had already died. It had been his wish to be buried in these peaceful grounds on the estate that had been in his family for so many generations. This rural resting-place was appropriate for a man who basically had simple tastes and did not wish for an ornate tomb or for a memorial place in Westminster Abbey, as some had hoped and thought he deserved.

But before this the nation had insisted upon a service in the Abbey where high and low could meet to pay tribute. Blinds were drawn in the West End clubs and mansions. Mourners presented an amazing social mix. There were great statesmen, both those who had supported him and those who had opposed him, alongside many poor people, mostly wearing an armband of black ribbon, who went timidly into the great Abbey to give thanks for their noble friend.

There were also people from the two hundred organizations which Shaftesbury had served so faithfully. An odd crowd indeed – costermongers with their musicians, shoe-blacks and flower-girls, boys from the sailing ships and hundreds of ordinary men and women who had reason to thank God for Shaftesbury and his battles on their behalf.

It poured with rain on the day of the service but this did not stop mourners from attending and waiting about. The funeral hearse, drawn by four black horses, was very plain. What a contrast to the funeral of Wellington which had so upset Shaftesbury. And what a contrast also to that unspeakable pauper funeral party which had so horrified the young Shaftesbury as a boy of fourteen and which had probably fixed the direction for his life.

Tributes poured in from all over the world. And the poor people themselves cherished their personal memories of one who had been noble lord but also friend. Was he not the aristocrat who had taken an old woman into his carriage because she looked so weary, and accompanied a small girl across the road because she took his hand and said, "You have such a kind face"?

The children of public figures like Shaftesbury are sometimes less than appreciative of their father's efforts. But the sons of the Earl and his daughter and descendants could truly say they would miss him. They joined with the rest of the nation in acknowledging his character. Cecil Ashley was deeply moved at his father's funeral to see the crowds lining the damp streets, many standing bare-headed in the rain to see the cortège enter the Abbey. He admitted, "I thought it was the most heart-stirring sight my eyes had ever looked upon."

After a year or two, subscriptions were invited to pay for a memorial to the people's friend. The inscription to this was written by another great statesman, William Gladstone, then Prime Minister. He penned several lines to the memory of Shaftesbury, ending with the words: "The Earl was a blessing to his people and a name to be by them ever gratefully remembered."

People tend to forget very easily, more so as the generations pass. But today in England's capital city there is still a Shaftesbury Society, a Shaftesbury Avenue, a Shaftesbury Estate, and in the middle of Piccadilly, the memorial itself. This is a fountain crowned by a classical figure of Eros, the boy-god of love.

Most passers-by have no idea why the little statue is there. They do not know that the man-

woman love it represents is but a shadow of
the all-embracing Christian love which the Earl
of Shaftesbury displayed in his energetic, unre-
lenting, constant pursuit of happiness for
underprivileged people.

His Christian faith was often stern, his sense
of duty strong, but the plight of pathetic
children and distressed men and women
brought out in him not only obedience to God's
will but also deep emotion for those he tried to
help. He could truly love them. And for them
he fought the fight, the fight for the poor.

If he were alive today he would surely say:
There is still much to be done – different
battles, but battles still – both here and elsewhere throughout the world. The cause of the
child and of the underprivileged is not yet
ended . . . It must go on.